CONTENTS

- 2 Numbers to 100
- 3 Counting
- 5 One More and One Less
- 6 Comparing Numbers
- 7 Value of Digits
- 8 Solving Number Problems
- 9 Adding and Taking Away to 10
- 10 Adding and Taking Away to 20
- 11 Addition and Subtraction
- 14 Part Whole Models
- 15 Finding the Inverse
- 16 Grouping and Arrays
- 17 2s, 5s and 10s
- 18 Odds and Evens
- 19 Multiplying and Dividing
- 21 Multiplication Problems
- 22 Division Problems
- 23 Finding a Half
- 24 Finding a Quarter
- 25 Fractions of Shapes
- 26 Fractions of Amounts
- 27 Equivalent Fractions
- 29 Measuring

- 30 Comparing Measurements
- 31 Money Values
- 32 Ordering Events in a Day
- 33 Days of the Week
- 34 Telling the Time
- 35 2D Shapes
- 36 Corners and Sides
- 37 3D Shapes
- 38 3D Shape Nets
- 39 2D and 3D Shapes
- 40 Position
- 41 Shape Patterns
- 42 Patterns
- 43 Direction and Movement
- 44 Pictograms and Tally Charts
- 45 Block Charts and Tables
- 46 Answers

ONLINE ACTIVITIES

On some of the pages you will see QR codes. These QR codes take you to online Purple Mash activities which support learning from the relevant page.

To use the QR codes, scan the QR code with the camera on your web enabled tablet, click on the link and the activity will appear on screen.

Alternatively, QR readers are available on the app store for your device.

Peanuts and all related titles, logos and characters are trademarks of Peanuts Worldwide LLC © 2024 Peanuts Worldwide LLC.

Created by SCHULZ

Published 2024. Little Brother Books Ltd, Ground Floor, 23 Southernhay East, Exeter, Devon EX1 1QL
books@littlebrotherbooks.co.uk | www.littlebrotherbooks.co.uk
Printed in the United Kingdom
The Little Brother Books trademark, email and website addresses, are the sole and exclusive properties of Little Brother Books Limited.

NUMBERS TO 100

Charlie and Sally are at the library counting the books they want to borrow. There are a lot of them! Can you help them count to 100?

1

Count from **1** to **100** using the hundred square, and where there is a number missing, write it in.

1	2	3	4	5	6	7	8		10
	12	13		15		17	18	19	
21	22	23	24	25	26		28	29	30
31		33	34		36	37	38	39	
41	42	43		45	46	47		49	50
51	52	53	54	55		57	58		60
61	62	63		65	66	67		69	70
71		73	74	75	76		78	79	
81	82	83	84	85	86	87	88	89	90
91	92	93		95	96	97	98		100

2

Sally has cut up the hundred square and wants you to fill in the missing numbers. Count along and write in what is missing. You can use the hundred square above to help if you need it.

a.

17	18		
27		29	
	38	39	40
		49	50

b.

31			34
		43	
51		53	
	62		

c.

	54		56
		65	
	74		
		84	
93			

COUNTING

Pig Pen has a packet of his favourite sweets, gum drops. He's counting how many he has so he can give them out to his friends.

1 Pig Pen wants to count how many of each different coloured gum drops he has. Can you help him?

a.

b.

c.

d.

Write the words to match the digits.

11 .... 4 ....

8 .... 19 ....

2 Charlie has helped Pig Pen to sort the gum drops into piles. Count the gum drops and draw a line to match each pile to the correct number. One has been done for you.

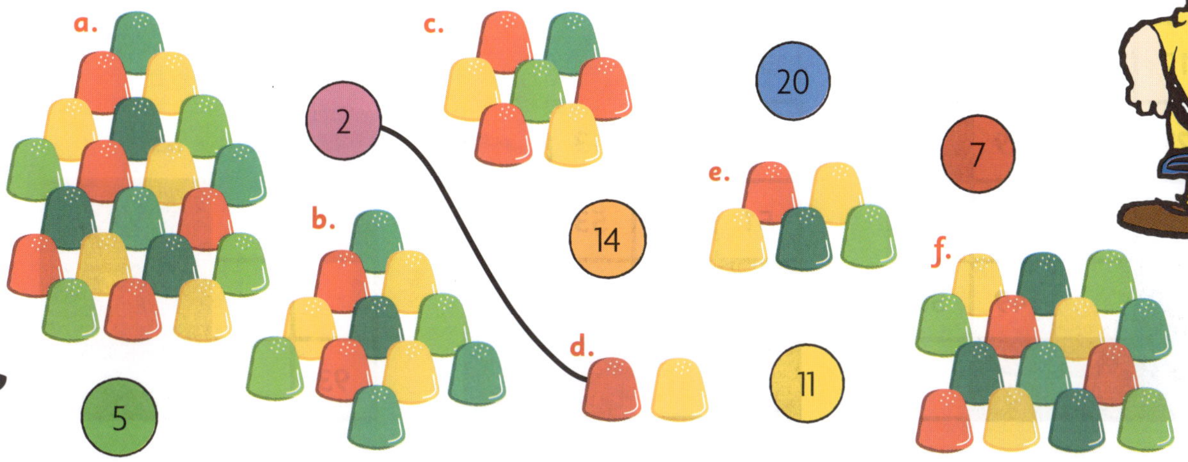

a.

b.

c.

d.

e.

f.

COUNTING

Marcie is sorting through the lost property box at school. Lots of people seem to have lost their hats!

1

Help Marcie sort through the lost property by looking at the different amounts and drawing the correct number of hats.

 **a. 8** yellow hats

 **b. 5** blue hats

 **c. 3** pink hats

 **d. 4** orange hats

2

Marcie has found something of Charlie's in the lost property box. Can you join the dots to reveal what it is? Make sure you count the dots in order.

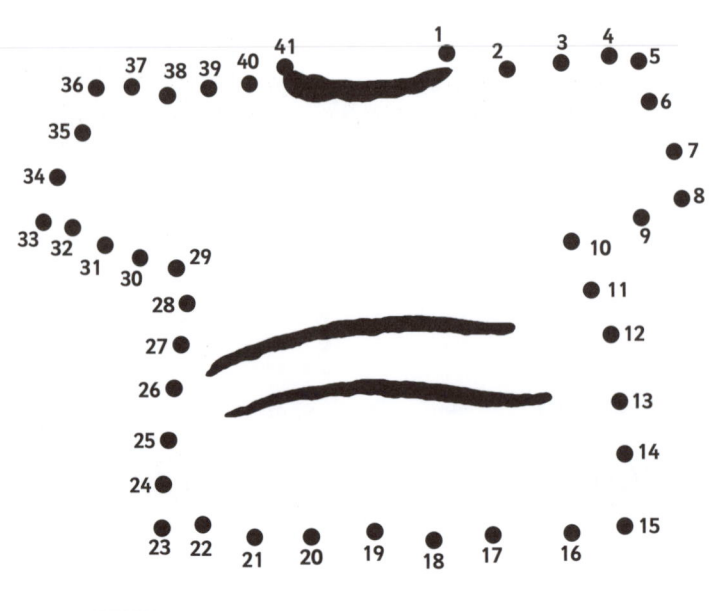

ONE MORE AND ONE LESS

It's lunchtime and the school canteen is busy. Charlie and his friends are choosing their food but they keep changing their minds and altering their orders by adding things or taking them off. Can you help sort the orders out?

1 Count the number of food types and write down one more and one less than the number shown in the pictures. The first one has been done for you.

		One more	One less
a.	(6 sandwiches)	7	5
b.	(8 drinks)		
c.	(4 hot dogs)		
d.	(5 pizzas)		

2 While everyone eats their lunch, can you match each sentence to the correct answer?

a. 1 more than 5 is   0

b. 1 less than 12 is   11

c. 1 more than 19 is   15

d. 1 less than 1 is   6

e. 1 more than 14 is   20

COMPARING NUMBERS

Lucy runs a psychiatry booth charging 5 cents for advice. She's had a busy day and is counting up the money she's made.

1 Look at the numbers and write them in the boxes in order from smallest to largest.

1   11   21   4   19   8

☐ ☐ ☐ ☐ ☐ ☐

2 Can you help Lucy compare the numbers below? Use the symbols to help.

< means less than   > means greater than   = means same as

Remember, the arrow always points to the smaller number. For example, 4 < 5

a. 14 ☐ 10

b. 17 ☐ 17

c. 3 ☐ 9

d. 8 ☐ 16

e. 20 ☐ 3

VALUE OF DIGITS

Snoopy's favourite drink is root beer so Charlie's trying to make some homemade root beer for his friend. The recipe is very confusing though! Can you help Charlie work out the numbers next to the ingredients?

25 =

tens	ones
2	5

20 + 5

The number 25 is made up of 2 tens and 5 ones.

1 How many tens and ones are in these numbers?

a. 65 = ☐ tens and ☐ ones

b. 42 = ☐ tens and ☐ ones

c. 38 = ☐ tens and ☐ ones

d. 13 = ☐ ten and ☐ ones

e. 26 = ☐ tens and ☐ ones

2 What number do these tens and ones make?

a. 3 tens and 2 ones = ☐

b. 7 tens and 5 ones = ☐

c. 4 tens and 9 ones = ☐

d. 5 tens and 1 one = ☐

e. 1 ten and 7 ones = ☐

3 The digits in these numbers represent tens and ones. Add the numbers together and write the new number. The first one has been done for you.

a. 30 spoons of sugar + 4 spoons of sugar = **34** spoons of sugar

b. 10 grammes of molasses + 7 grammes of molasses = ☐ grammes of molasses

c. 20 pints of water + 5 pints of water = ☐ pints of water

d. 40 grammes of roots + 9 grammes of roots = ☐ grammes of roots

7

SOLVING NUMBER PROBLEMS

Sally has come up with a way to boost her pocket money. She's set up a sweet stall outside her house and is selling sweets in boxes of 10 as well as single sweets.

10 + 10 + 3 = 23 sweets

1 Write down the number of sweets there are in each image below.

a.

b.

c.

d.

2 Which of Sally's statements are correct? Tick true or false for each one.

                                                               True False

a. 4 boxes and 3 sweets make 43 sweets.

b. 54 is bigger than 6 tens and 1 one.

c. 20 is the same as 1 ten and 2 ones.

d. 10 tens can be written as 100.

e. Five more than 85 is 91.

ADDING AND TAKING AWAY TO 10

Charlie is making cupcakes for a bake sale at school but Snoopy keeps swiping them! Charlie needs to make sure he still has enough cupcakes to sell.

1 Work out how many cupcakes Charlie has baked. Draw the cupcakes to help you.

 4 cupcakes + 1 cupcake =  5 cupcakes

a. 6 + 2 =

b. 7 + 3 =

c. 5 + 3 =

2 The icing from the cupcakes has splattered everywhere and has hidden some of the numbers. Work out the numbers that have been hidden by icing splats to make the questions correct.

a. 3 +  = 5   b. + 1 = 10   c. 5 + 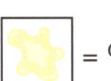 = 9   d.  + 3 = 7

3 Every time Snoopy swipes a cupcake, one is subtracted, or taken away, from Charlie's total.

6 - 4 = 2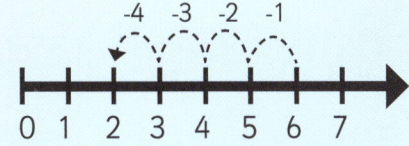

Answer the questions below by counting backwards along the number line.

a. 7 - 4 =   b. 9 - 2 =   c. 4 - 2 =   d. 7 - 3 =

ADDING AND TAKING AWAY TO 20

Charlie and his classmates are helping their teacher, Miss Othmar, organise the stationery cupboard. Before they can make it look neat and tidy, Miss Othmar wants to know how many of each item is in the cupboard.

1

Can you help count the pens? Use the number line to help you.

a. 13 + 6 =
b. 8 + 7 =
c. 14 + 2 =
d. 9 + 3 =

e. 7 - 6 =
f. 15 - 5 =
g. 12 - 7 =
h. 19 - 10 =

2

There are lots more pencils than pens in the stationery cupboard so the numbers are larger. Number bonds to 10 can help us answer questions with larger numbers.

8 + 2 = 10   **so**   80 + 20 = 100

Use this method to fill in the gaps and work out the missing numbers.

a. 6 + ☐ = 10   so   60 + ☐ = 100

b. ☐ + 8 = 10   so   ☐ + 80 = 100

c. ☐ + 3 = 10   so   ☐ + 30 = 100

d. 5 + ☐ = 10   so   50 + ☐ = 100

e. ☐ + 9 = 10   so   ☐ + 90 = 100

ADDITION AND SUBTRACTION

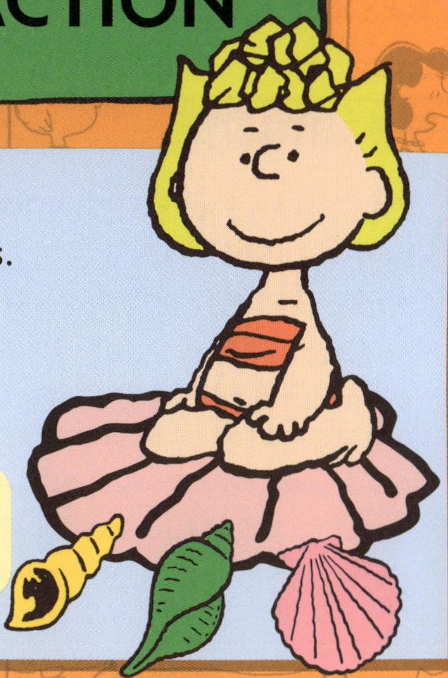

The Brown family are enjoying a daytrip to the beach. Sally and Charlie have collected lots of shells. They are adding together the numbers to see how many they have. Can you help them before Snoopy causes mischief?

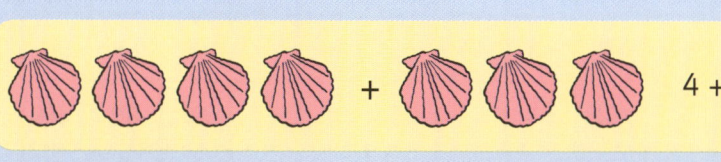 4 + 3 = 7

1 Draw a line to match the number of shells that Sally and Charlie have collected with the correct total number.

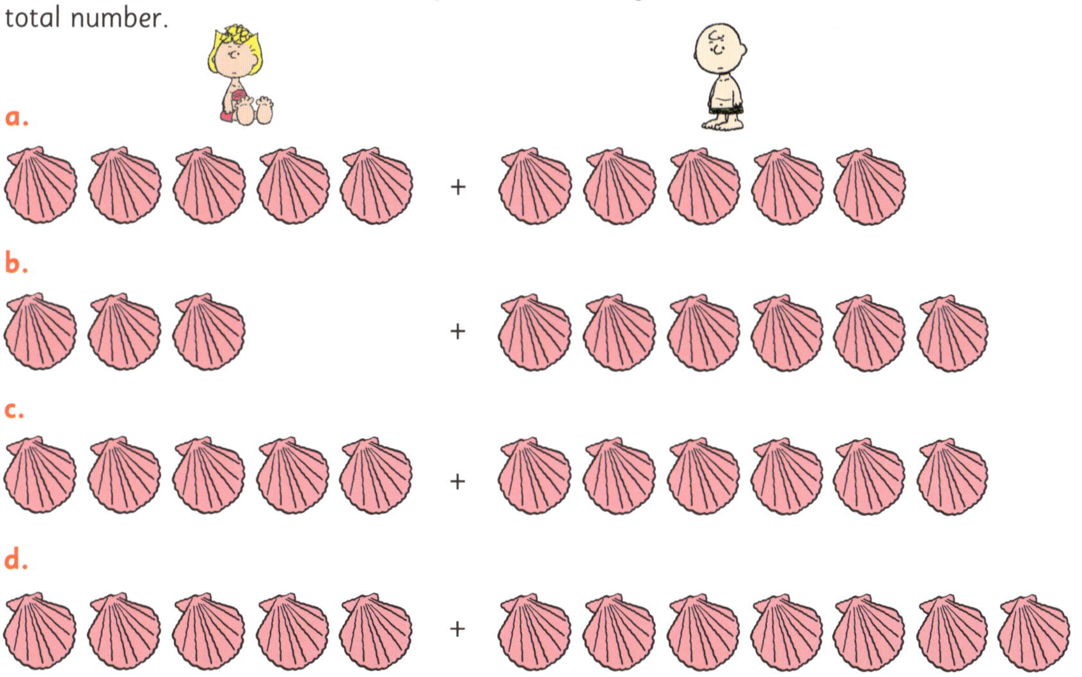

a.  +    9

b.  +    12

c.  + 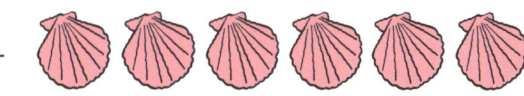   10

d.  + 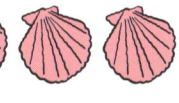   11

2 Snoopy is digging in the sand and has accidentally buried some of the shells! Work out how many are left now.

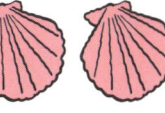

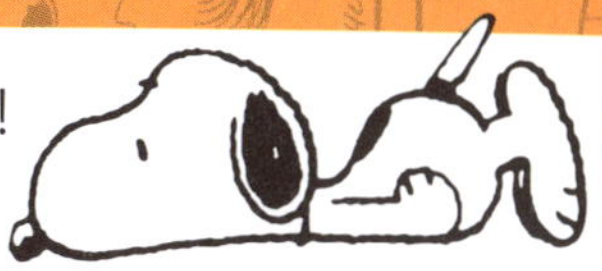

a. 10 - 7 = ☐   b. 10 - 4 = ☐   c. 9 - 5 = ☐   d. 8 - 6 = ☐

11

ADDITION AND SUBTRACTION

Pig Pen is trying to do his maths homework but his maths book is covered in dirty fingerprints and he can't see all the numbers! Use the number square to help him work out which numbers are missing from the sums below.

1	2	3	4	5	6	7	8	9	10
11	12	13	14	15	16	17	18	19	20
21	22	23	24	25	26	27	28	29	30
31	32	33	34	35	36	37	38	39	40
41	42	43	44	45	46	47	48	49	50
51	52	53	54	55	56	57	58	59	60
61	62	63	64	65	66	67	68	69	70
71	72	73	74	75	76	77	78	79	80
81	82	83	84	85	86	87	88	89	90
91	92	93	94	95	96	97	98	99	100

1

21 +  = 43. To find the missing number, you could count how many jumps it is from 21 to 43.

It takes 22 jumps from 21 to land on 43. So, 21 + **22** = 43

These number sentences use adding.

a. 10 + ◯ = 19   b. ◯ + 21 = 46   c. 17 + ◯ = 32

d. ◯ + 12 = 20   e. 34 + ◯ = 43   f. 21 + ◯ = 52

2

30 − ◯ = 12. To find the missing number, you could count how many jumps back it is from 30 to 12.

It takes 18 jumps back from 30 to land on 12. So, 30 − **18** = 12

These number sentences use take away.

a. 27 − ◯ = 15   b. 48 − ◯ = 36   c. 37 − ◯ = 29

d. 14 − ◯ = 7   e. 22 − ◯ = 18   f. ◯ − 13 = 21

ADDITION AND SUBTRACTION

Can you solve the sums to lead sleepy Snoopy back to his kennel so he can have a nap?

1 Complete the number sentences to help Snoopy get to his kennel.

a. 14 + 3 =

b. 9 + 9 =

c. 15 + 4 =

d. 12 + 7 =

e. 17 + 6 =

f. 26 + 30 =

g. 35 + 20 =

h. 12 + 50 =

i. 23 + 40 =

j. 36 + 10 =

PART WHOLE MODELS

Miss Othmar gives out gold stars at school for good behaviour. Today, lots of pupils in her class are trying to win gold stars. Who do you think will get some?

1 Help Miss Othmar count the gold stars before she hands them out.

These are part whole models; the whole is at the top and it is split into 2 parts.

a. 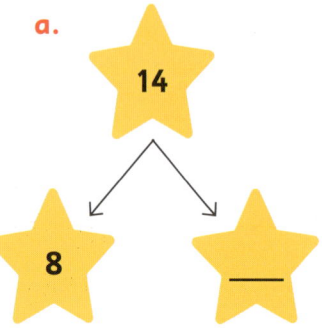 b.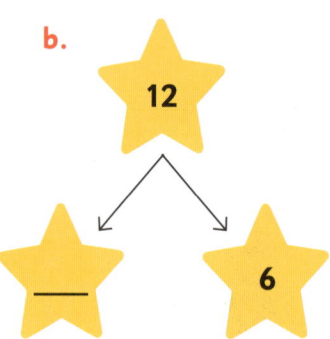

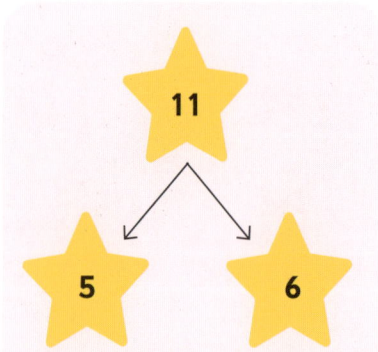

c. 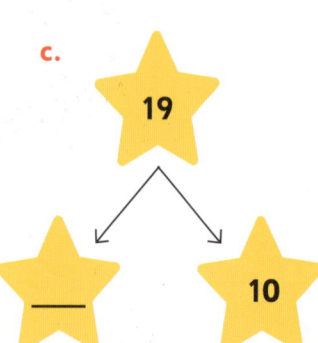 d.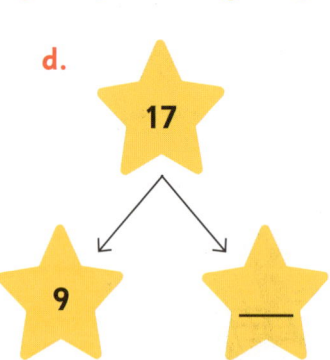

2 Linus was awarded 11 gold stars in the morning and 8 gold stars in the afternoon. How many gold stars did he get altogether?

3 Pig Pen was awarded 13 gold stars for neat handwriting but then he got dirty fingerprints all over his work so Miss Othmar took away 5. How many were left?

4 Schroeder was awarded 9 gold stars for doing his homework and 9 more for following the school rules. How many did he get in total?

FINDING THE INVERSE

Peppermint Patty loves sports of all kinds and is always on the go. Marcie has convinced her that as well as exercising her body, she needs to give her brain a work out. To do this, she's been trying to solve some maths problems as quickly as she can.

Peppermint Patty realises that if you know that 4 + 5 = 9 then it takes no time at all to work out that 5 + 4 = 9. She can quickly swap the numbers over to work out subtraction questions too so 9 − 5 = 4 and 9 − 4 = 5.

1 Use these number facts to fill in the missing answers.

a. 3 + 6 = 9   so   9 - 6 = ☐

b. 10 + 5 = 15   so   15 - ☐ = 10

c. 20 - 8 = 12   so   8 + ☐ = 20

d. 13 + 3 = 16   so   16 - 3 = ☐

e. 14 - 5 = 9   so   ☐ + 9 = 14

2 Have a go at writing the number sentences about these fact families.

a. 12   4   16

___ + ___ = ___   ___ + ___ = ___   ___ − ___ = ___   ___ − ___ = ___

b. 10   7   17

___ + ___ = ___   ___ + ___ = ___   ___ − ___ = ___   ___ − ___ = ___

c. 14   6   20

___ + ___ = ___   ___ + ___ = ___   ___ − ___ = ___   ___ − ___ = ___

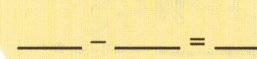

GROUPING AND ARRAYS

Charlie and Snoopy are playing in the snow. Snowflakes keep landing on Snoopy's nose and making him sneeze but they quickly melt so it's OK! Charlie wants to work out the total amount of snowflakes that land each time by grouping them together.

1 We count in groups when we multiply and multiple snowflakes are landing on Snoopy's nose at once. Work out the total number of snowflakes below.

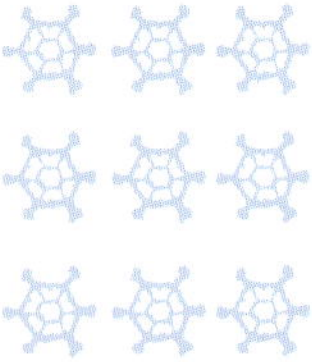

a. 3 groups of 3 = ☐

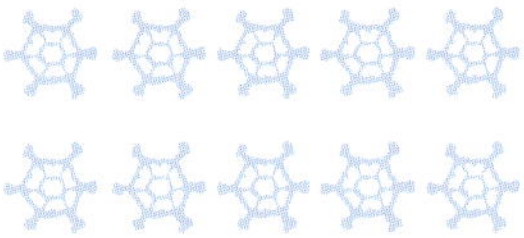

b. 2 groups of 5 = ☐

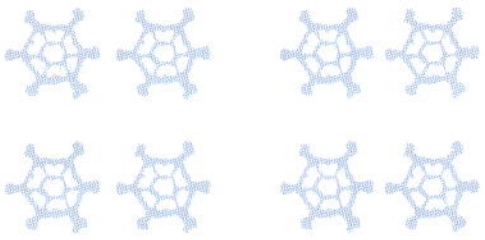

c. 4 groups of 2 = ☐

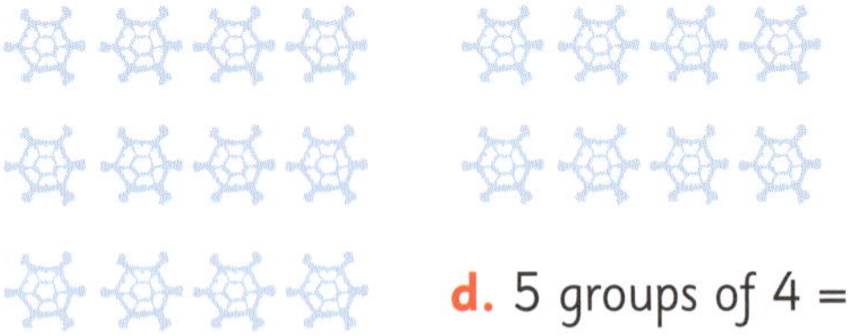

d. 5 groups of 4 = ☐

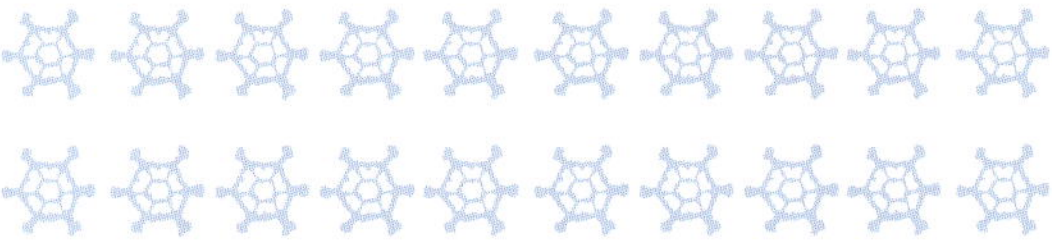

e. 2 groups of 10 = ☐

2 Now Charlie and Snoopy are having a snowball fight! Charlie wants to know how many snowballs he's made. He uses arrays to help him multiply. Try these:

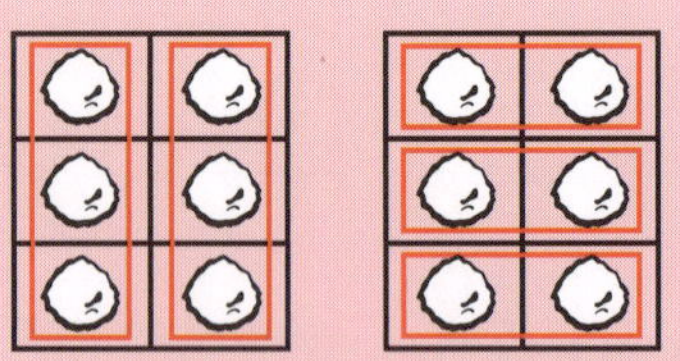

Charlie could interpret these arrays as 2 groups of 3 snowballs (2 x 3) or 3 groups of 2 snowballs (3 x 2). Both arrays show a total of 6 snowballs.

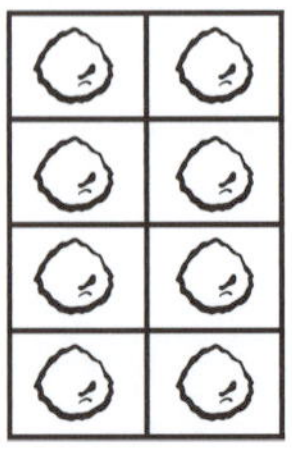

a. 2 x 4 = ☐
4 x 2 = ☐

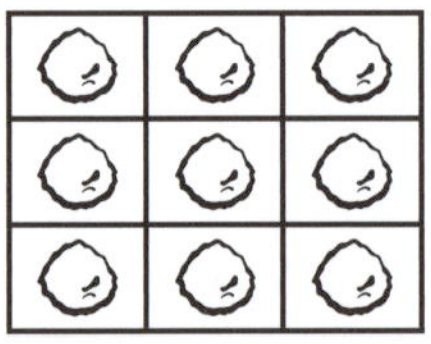

b. 3 x 3 = ☐

c. 2 x 7 = ☐
7 x 2 = ☐

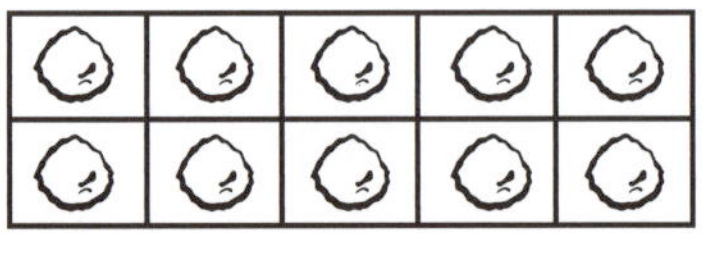

d. 5 x 2 = ☐
2 x 5 = ☐

16

2s, 5s AND 10s

Peppermint Patty has some multiplication homework to do before she can go and play baseball. Can you help her complete it so she can get out on the pitch as quickly as possible?

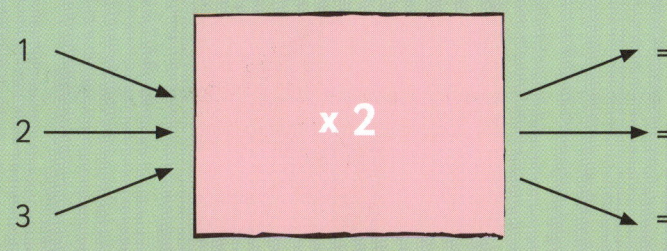

1 Fill in the missing numbers to multiply these numbers by 2. The first one has been done for you.

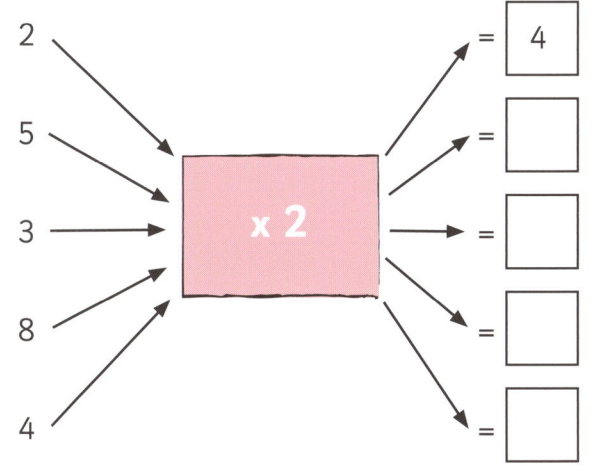

2 Now multiply the numbers by 5.

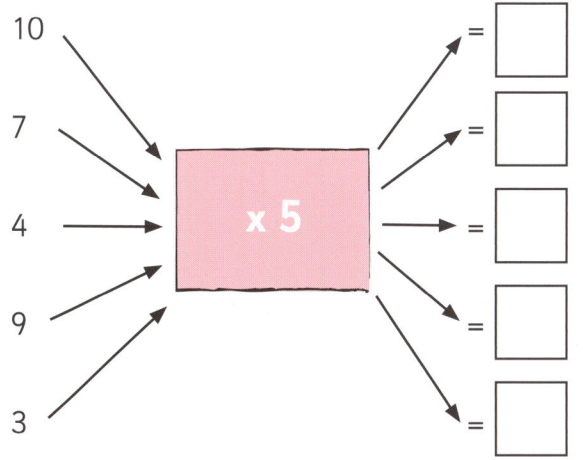

3 Peppermint Patty has rushed the last question in her hurry to play baseball and has got some of the answers wrong. Fix the wrong answers by writing the correct numbers in the boxes.

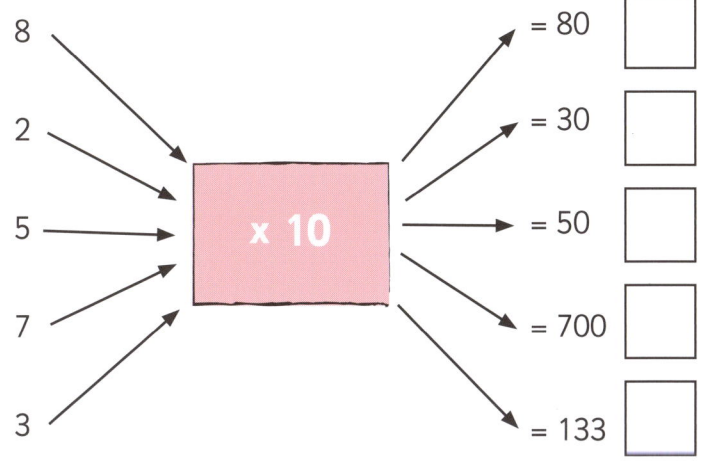

ODDS AND EVENS

Miss Othmar is teaching an art lesson at school. Pig Pen is a messy painter and he's accidentally flicked some paint on the odd and even number lines hanging on the wall! The pupils use the lines to work out which numbers are odd and which are even.

1 Complete these number lines with odd and even numbers.

a.

2 ⬤ 6 8 ⬤ 12 ⬤ ⬤ 18 ⬤

b.

⬤ 3 ⬤ 7 9 ⬤ ⬤ 15 ⬤ 19

2 Are all of these numbers in the right box? Circle any that are incorrect.

ODD

15	6	5
1	3	17	5
7	1	12

EVEN

1	6	4	8
2	11	7	10

3 Use your knowledge of odd and even numbers to join the dots to reveal each picture.

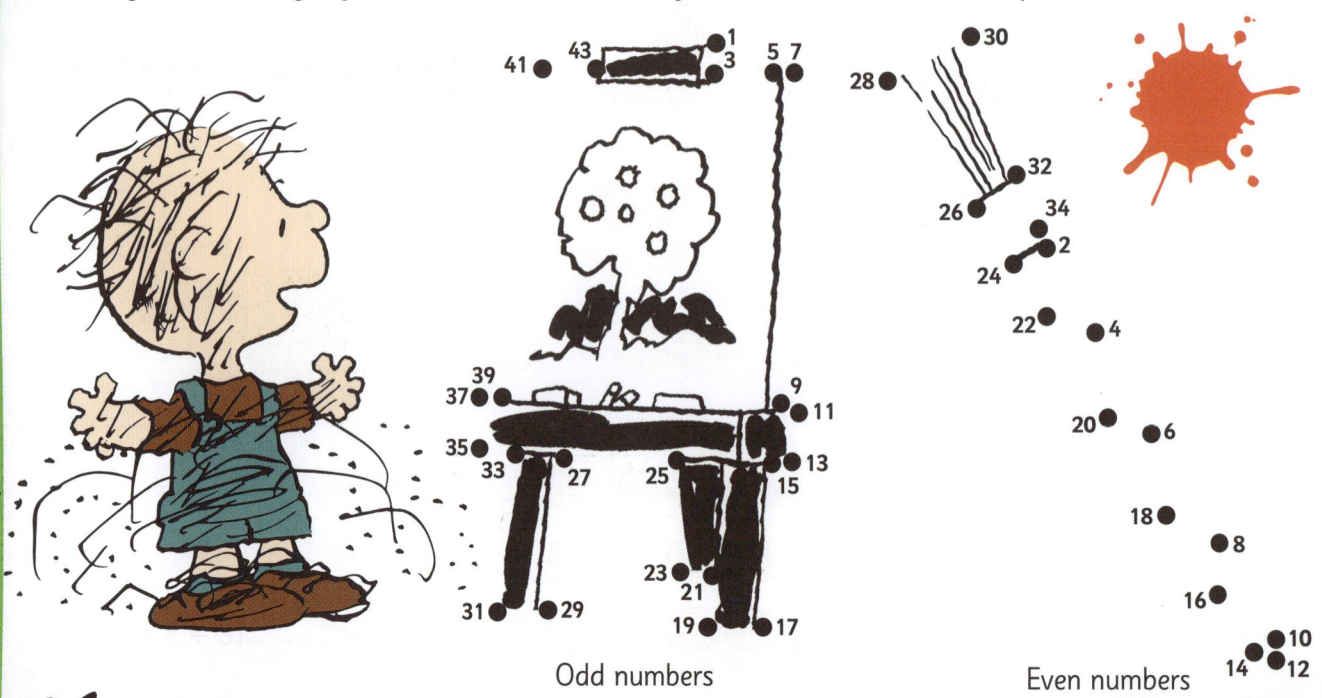

Odd numbers   Even numbers

MULTIPLYING AND DIVIDING

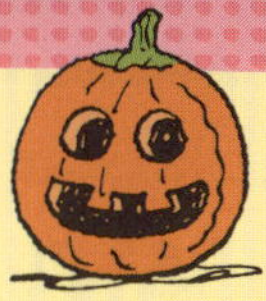

It's Halloween and lots of people have bought pumpkins. Charlie is using multiplication and division to work out how many he's seen while out trick or treating. He knows how closely related multiplication and division are.

1 Match each multiplication number sentence with the correct diagram and division number sentence. The first one has been done for you.

3 x 2 = 6   a.    8 ÷ 2 = 4

3 x 5 = 15   b.    6 ÷ 2 = 3

4 x 2 = 8   c. 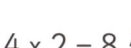   9 ÷ 3 = 3

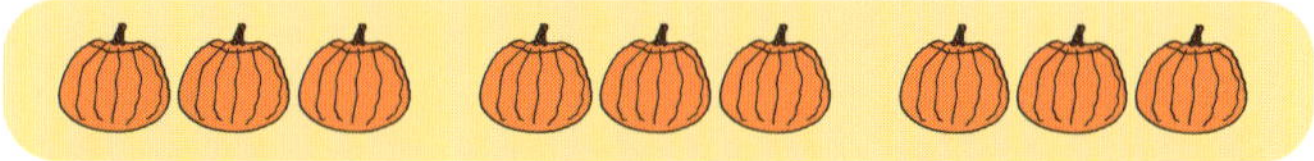

5 x 5 = 25   d.   25 ÷ 5 = 5

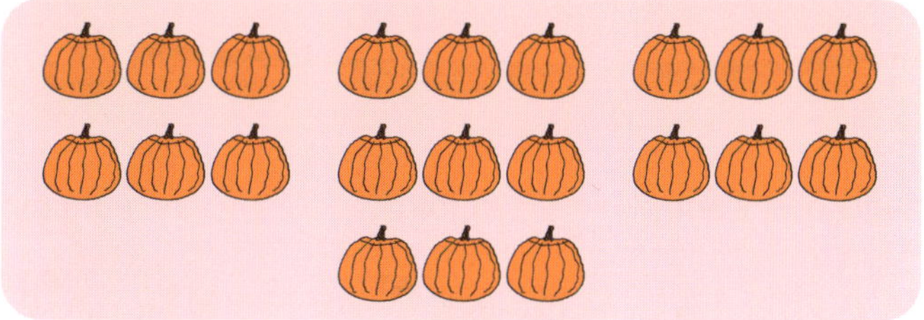

6 x 3 = 18   e.   15 ÷ 5 = 3

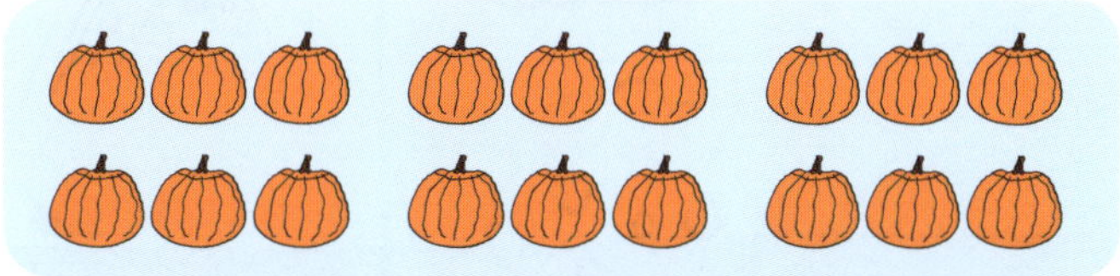

7 x 3 = 21   f.    21 ÷ 3 = 7

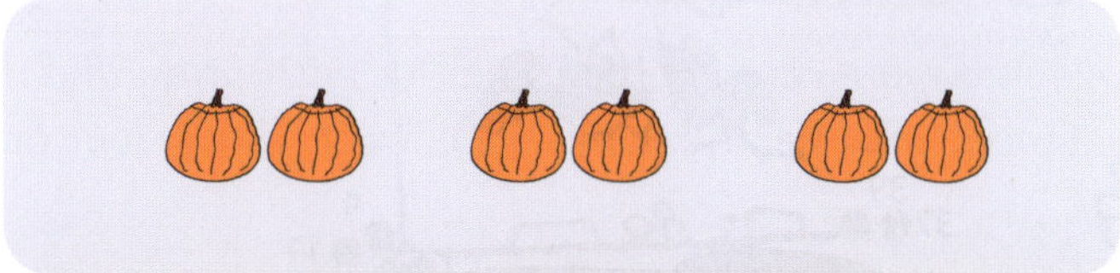

3 x 3 = 9   g.    18 ÷ 3 = 6

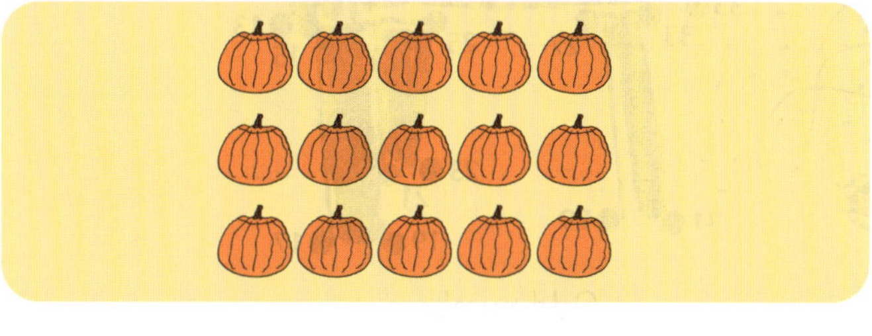

MULTIPLYING AND DIVIDING

Snoopy has worked out that he can sledge down the hill two different ways and get the same result – reaching the bottom! That works with multiplication and division too.

An array is an arrangement of rows and columns that match a multiplication. We can write multiplication and division facts for them like the example here:

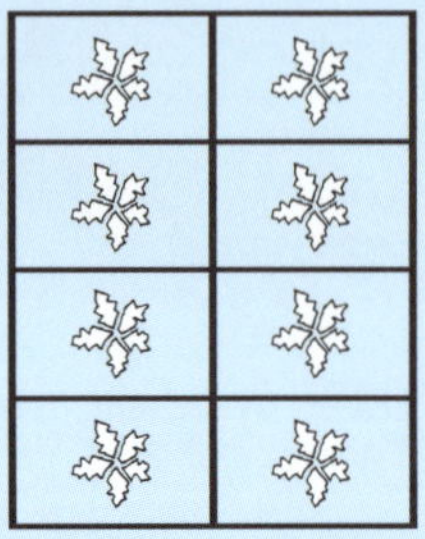

2 x 4 = 8
4 x 2 = 8
8 ÷ 2 = 4
8 ÷ 4 = 2

1 Write the multiplication and division facts for these arrays of snowballs.

a.

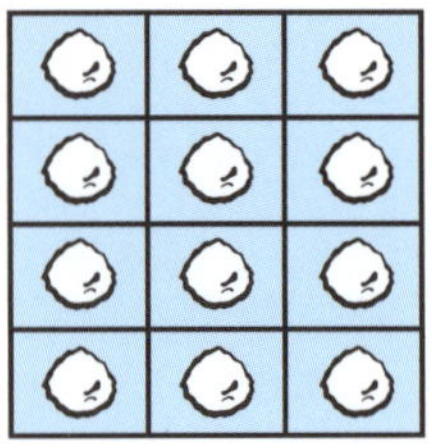

____ x ____ = ____
____ x ____ = ____
____ ÷ ____ = ____
____ ÷ ____ = ____

c.

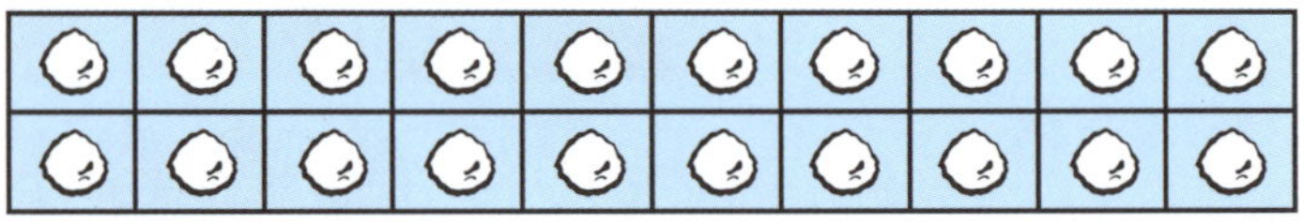

____ x ____ = ____   ____ ÷ ____ = ____
____ x ____ = ____   ____ ÷ ____ = ____

b.

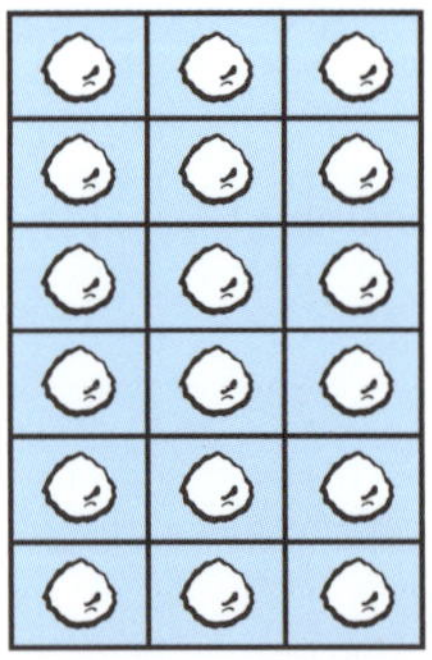

____ x ____ = ____
____ x ____ = ____
____ ÷ ____ = ____
____ ÷ ____ = ____

2 Division needs to be done in a more careful order. Look at each array and decide which of the two division number sentences underneath it could be correct. Circle your answer.

a.

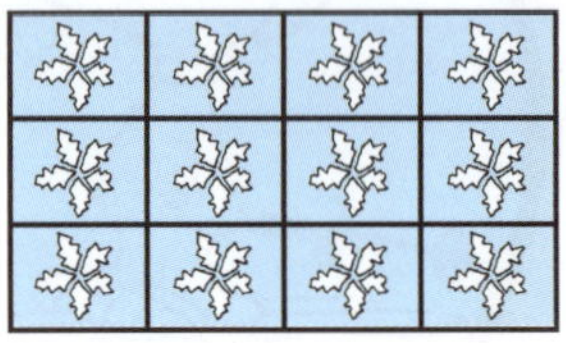

12 ÷ 3 = 4
4 ÷ 4 = 16

b.

1 ÷ 3 = 1
3 ÷ 1 = 3

c.

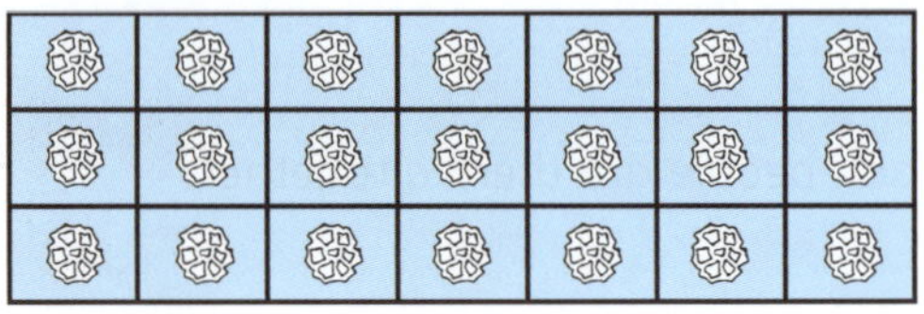

21 ÷ 7 = 3
3 ÷ 24 = 8

20

MULTIPLICATION PROBLEMS

Peppermint Patty is the fastest thrower around! Can you solve these problems faster than Peppermint Patty can throw an American football? Ready, get set, go!

1 Using your 2, 5 and 10 times tables, answer these questions.

a. 5 x 3 = ☐   b. 10 x 10 = ☐   c. 8 x 5 = ☐   d. 2 x 1 = ☐

e. 7 x 2 = ☐   f. 3 x 2 = ☐   g. 9 x 10 = ☐   h. 5 x 5 = ☐

2 Peppermint Patty is wondering if she can be even faster with her throws if she throws multiple balls at once, using multiplication instead of adding repeatedly.

5 + 5 + 5 = 3 x 5 = 15

Turn these repeated addition number sentences into multiplication to show how much faster she could be!

a. 3 + 3 + 3 = 9
☐ x ☐ = ☐

b. 4 + 4 = 8
☐ x ☐ = ☐

c. 10 + 10 + 10 + 10 = 40
☐ x ☐ = ☐

d. 2 + 2 + 2 + 2 + 2 = 10
☐ x ☐ = ☐

3

a. Snoopy goes skiing for 10 minutes a day for 3 days. How many minutes does he spend skiing altogether? ☐

b. 5 groups of 8 people are having a huge snowball fight. How many people are there altogether? ☐

c. Charlie Brown has 9 pairs of gloves in his drawer. How many gloves does he have altogether? ☐

DIVISION PROBLEMS

Snoopy is cooking in the kitchen and wants to divide the food with Charlie Brown. He's made eight pancakes, as he knows Charlie loves them, and wants to share half with him.

So, eight divided between Snoopy and Charlie means they get four each (8 ÷ 2 = 4).

1 Use your number facts to solve these division questions.

a. 8 ÷ 2 =   b. 35 ÷ 5 =   c. 12 ÷ 2 =

d. 10 ÷ 5 =   e. 100 ÷ 10 =   f. 20 ÷ 5 =

g. 50 ÷ 10 =   h. 18 ÷ 2 =   i. 30 ÷ 10 =

2 Peppermint Patty and Marcie are sharing 10 grapes.

How many do they each have?

3 Miss Othmar is sorting 20 pencils into 4 jars.

How many pencils are in each jar?

4 Sally needs 50 envelopes for her Christmas cards. The envelopes come in packs of 5.

How many packs does she need to buy?

5 Pig Pen has bought 50 gum drops and put them into boxes of 10.

How many gum drops are in each box?

FINDING A HALF

It's dinnertime at the Brown's house. Charlie and Sally are sharing out the food. They need to split everything in half, this means two equal parts, so that it is fair and they both get the same.

We can write a half like this: $\frac{1}{2}$

1 Find which of these burgers is cut in half and draw a circle around it. Remember that a half is 2 equal parts.

2 Sally is trying to cut this pizza in half to share. Can you help her? Draw a line through the pizza to cut it into two equal parts.

3 Sally knows that she can share things out into 2 equal piles to find half of an amount. Now that they've finished their dinner, she has some sweets to share with Charlie. Can you help Sally find half of these amounts of sweets?

a. $\frac{1}{2}$ of 4 = ☐   b. $\frac{1}{2}$ of 10 = ☐   c. $\frac{1}{2}$ of 6 = ☐   d. $\frac{1}{2}$ of 12 = ☐

FINDING A QUARTER

Schroeder is having a birthday party and his friends have come to celebrate with him. There are four of them so everything needs to be split into four equal parts.

These are called quarters and we can write a quarter like this: $\frac{1}{4}$

1 Which of these birthday cakes is cut into quarters? Draw a circle around it.

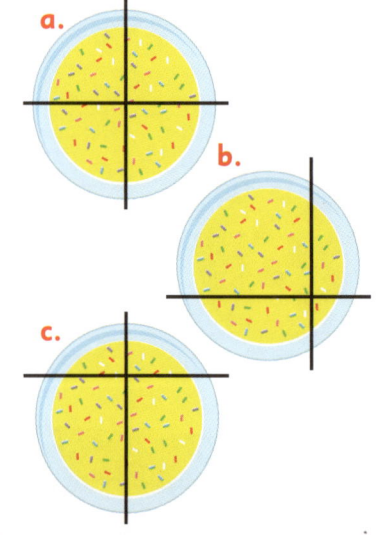

a.
b.
c.

2 Schroeder wants to share doughnuts between himself and his three friends at the party. Colour in a quarter of the doughnuts.

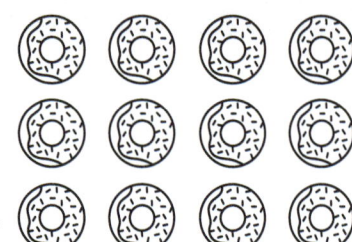

3 Schroeder knows that to share out the slices of cake into quarters, he needs to split them into 4 equal groups. While he is playing party games, have a go at finding a quarter of these amounts to see how many slices of cake each person will get.

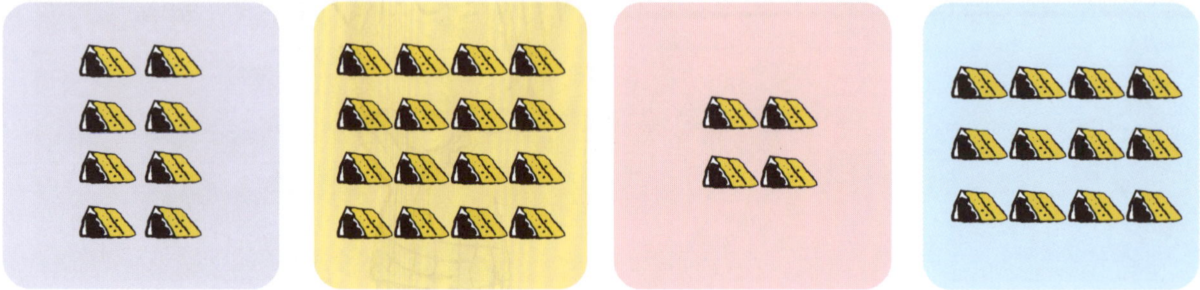

a. $\frac{1}{4}$ of 8 = ☐   b. $\frac{1}{4}$ of 16 = ☐   c. $\frac{1}{4}$ of 4 = ☐   d. $\frac{1}{4}$ of 12 = ☐

FRACTIONS OF SHAPES

Fractions are parts of a whole. When we write fractions, we think about how many parts the whole has been split in to. Peppermint Patty has been playing football and knows the football pitch is split into 2 halves.

We can write a half as: $\frac{1}{2}$

1 The pitch has been divided into two halves. Colour in one half.

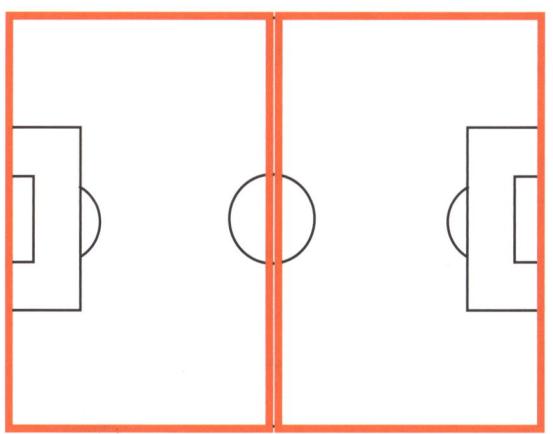

2 Peppermint Patty also likes to swim, and the pool is split into 4 equal parts. These are called quarters. We can write a quarter as $\frac{1}{4}$.

Colour in $\frac{1}{4}$ of the swimming pool.

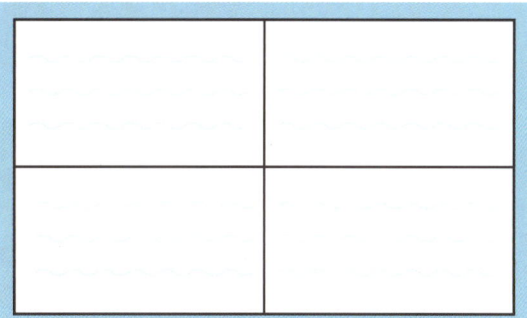

3 Peppermint Patty really likes playing netball, and the court is split into 3 equal parts, called thirds.

Colour in $\frac{1}{3}$ of the netball court.

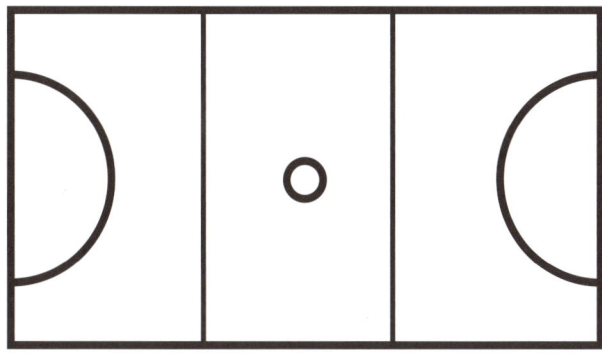

FRACTIONS OF AMOUNTS

The Peanuts gang are having a barbecue. They've cooked lots of burgers to share out between everybody. Snoopy can't wait to eat his and maybe someone else's as well!

1 Circle the correct number of burgers for each of the fractions below and write the answers in the boxes. The first one has been done for you.

a. $\frac{1}{2}$ of 10 = 5

b. $\frac{1}{4}$ of 8 =

c. $\frac{2}{4}$ of 8 =

d. $\frac{3}{4}$ of 8 =

e. $\frac{1}{2}$ of 4 =

f. $\frac{1}{4}$ of 4 =

g. $\frac{2}{4}$ of 4 =

2 So far, the friends have only eaten a fraction of the burgers that have been cooked. Can you work out the correct answer for each of these fractions of burgers?

a. $\frac{1}{2}$ of 6 =

b. $\frac{1}{4}$ of 20 =

c. $\frac{1}{3}$ of 12 =

d. $\frac{1}{2}$ of 16 =

e. $\frac{1}{4}$ of 8 =

f. $\frac{1}{3}$ of 18 =

EQUIVALENT FRACTIONS

Miss Othmar always has a different amount of children in her class as not all of them turn up every day. Today, only half of her students are present.

Half can be written in lots of different ways. $\frac{1}{2}$ is the same as $\frac{2}{4}$ and $\frac{4}{8}$.

1 Colour half of these shapes and write the equivalent fraction.

a. $\frac{1}{2} = \frac{\square}{4}$    b. $\frac{1}{2} = \frac{\square}{6}$

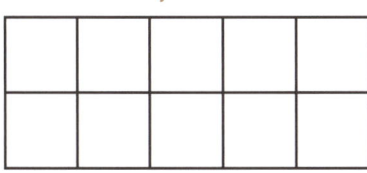

c. $\frac{1}{2} = \frac{\square}{10}$

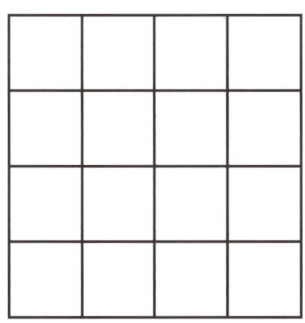

d. $\frac{1}{2} = \frac{\square}{16}$

2 On a very quiet day, Miss Othmar only has $\frac{1}{4}$ of the seats of her classroom filled.

Draw a circle around the shapes that have $\frac{1}{4}$ coloured in.

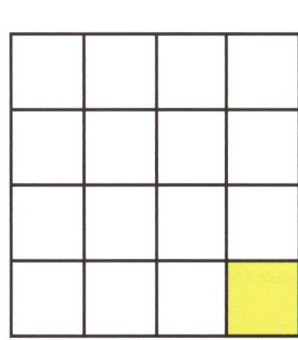
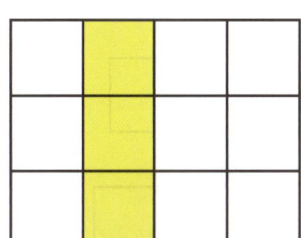

EQUIVALENT FRACTIONS

Linus has some bubble gum to share with his friends. There isn't enough for everyone to have a piece so he's using fractions to divide the bubble gum up.

1 Use the fraction wall to find the equivalent fractions.

a. $\frac{1}{2} = \frac{\square}{4}$ b. $\frac{2}{5} = \frac{\square}{10}$

c. $\frac{3}{6} = \frac{\square}{2}$ d. $\frac{3}{4} = \frac{\square}{8}$

e. $\frac{1}{3} = \frac{\square}{6}$ f. $\frac{2}{8} = \frac{\square}{4}$

1 whole										
1/2					1/2					
1/3				1/3				1/3		
1/4			1/4			1/4			1/4	
1/5		1/5		1/5		1/5		1/5	
1/6	1/6	1/6	1/6	1/6	1/6				
1/8	1/8	1/8	1/8	1/8	1/8	1/8	1/8		
1/10	1/10	1/10	1/10	1/10	1/10	1/10	1/10	1/10	1/10	
1/12	1/12	1/12	1/12	1/12	1/12	1/12	1/12	1/12	1/12	1/12	1/12

2 Draw a line to match the fractions that are the same.

a. $\frac{1}{2}$ $\frac{4}{6}$

b. $\frac{2}{3}$ $\frac{4}{10}$

c. $\frac{2}{5}$ $\frac{3}{12}$

d. $\frac{1}{4}$ $\frac{4}{8}$

3 Read the statements below then colour in the correct answers.

a. 6 out of 12 people had cherry flavour bubble gum. The fraction who had cherry flavour is:

$\boxed{\frac{1}{2}}$ $\boxed{\frac{1}{3}}$ $\boxed{\frac{1}{4}}$

b. 3 out of 12 people blew a big bubble. The fraction who blew a big bubble is:

$\boxed{\frac{1}{2}}$ $\boxed{\frac{1}{3}}$ $\boxed{\frac{1}{4}}$

c. 9 out of 12 people wanted more bubble gum. The fraction who wanted more bubble gum is:

$\boxed{\frac{1}{2}}$ $\boxed{\frac{1}{3}}$ $\boxed{\frac{1}{4}}$ $\boxed{\frac{3}{4}}$

MEASURING

Sally has been learning about measuring at school so she wants to measure the Brown's food at dinnertime. Hungry Charlie just wants to eat! Can you help Sally by answering the questions below?

1 Label the hotdogs to show which is **longer** and which is **shorter**.

a. _____   b. _____

2 Label the drinks to say which is **taller** and which is **shorter**.

a. _____   b. _____

3 Label these portions of chips to say which is **heavier** and which is **lighter**.

a. _____   b. _____

29

COMPARING MEASUREMENTS

Marcie has bought Peppermint Patty a present and is trying to work out which gift box is big enough to put it in.

Marcie needs to measure the width of the boxes in centimetres (we can write it as cm). Help her by reading the width from each ruler and writing it down.

1

The blue gift box is _____ cm wide.

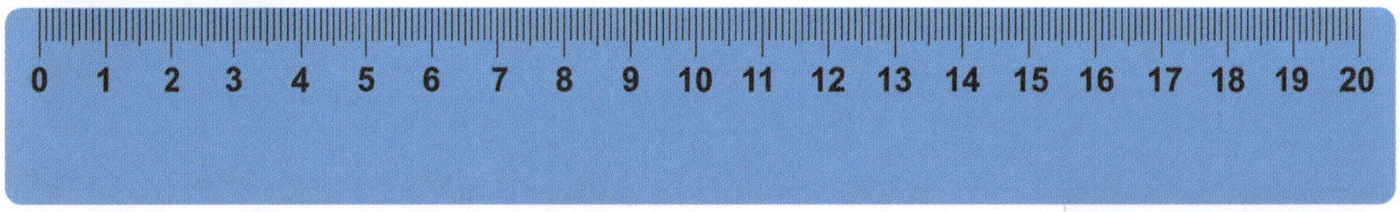

2

The red box is _____ cm wide.

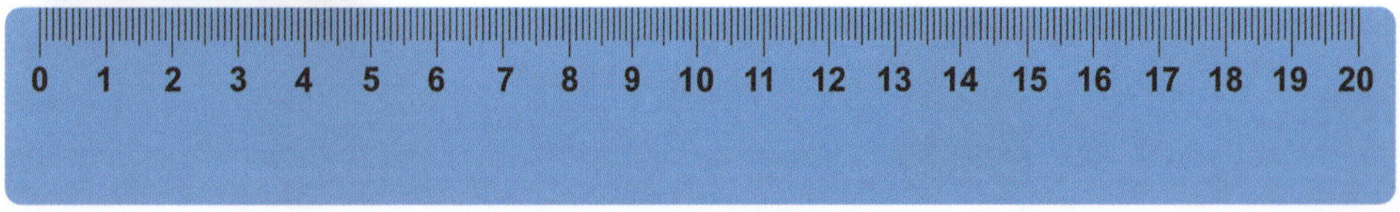

3 Which is wider: the blue gift box or the red gift box? _____

4

Marcie also wants to compare the weight of the two gift boxes. Read the weighing scales and write down how much each gift box weighs. We are using grammes and the symbol for this is g.

The blue gift box weighs _____ g.

The red gift box weighs _____ g.

Snoopy thinks the red gift box is heavier, is he right? _____

Blue gift box   Red gift box

MONEY VALUES

Sally loves Christmas and has set up a stall selling Christmas items, even though it's still a while away! Sally knows that 100 pennies make a pound. Sometimes we call pennies pence.

We can write this with symbols too. 100p = £1

1 Sally is finding different ways to make the same amounts of money. Match the pairs of amounts that make the same total. One has been done for you.

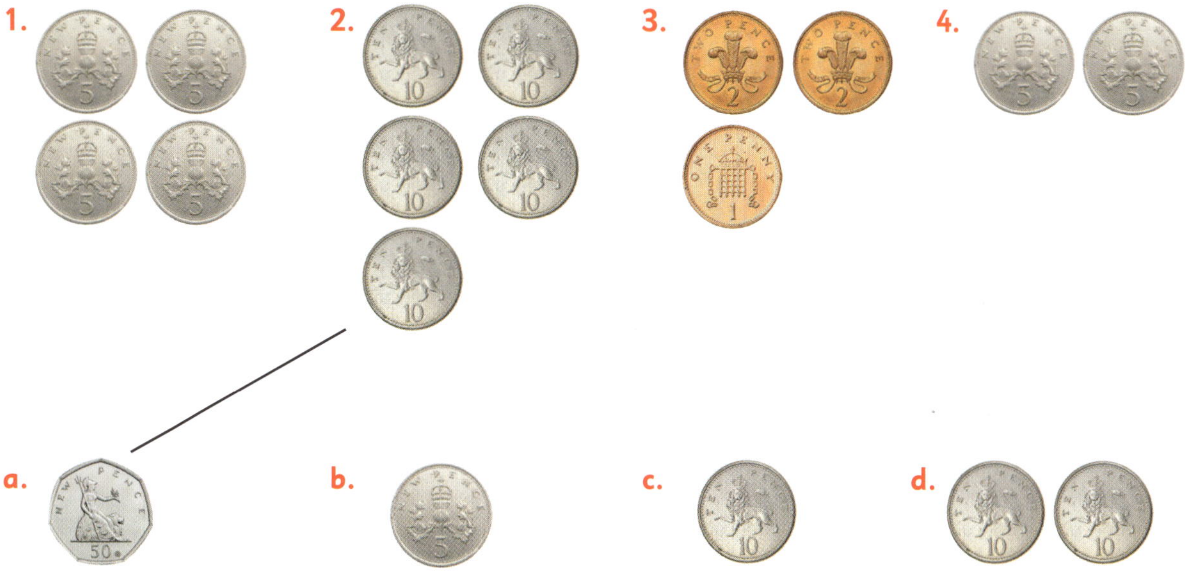

1.

2.

3.

4.

a.    b.    c.    d.

2 Sally needs to work out how much customers need to pay for their purchases, but she is very busy so needs some help.

a. Wreath   50p
   Christmas cracker 20p
   Wrapping paper   15p

   Total _____

b. Bow   30p
   Bauble   40p

   Total _____

c. Sweet   15p
   Candy cane   30p
   Wrapping paper 50p

   Total _____

ORDERING EVENTS IN A DAY

Charlie Brown has woken up early so he's decided to fly his kite before school. Do you think he can avoid the kite-eating tree this time?

1 Number the pictures to show the order of Charlie's morning events.

1. Charlie wakes up.
2. Charlie eats his breakfast.
3. Charlie checks the wind.
4. Charlie carries his kite to the park.
5. Charlie runs with his kite.
6. The kite ends up in the kite-eating tree.

2 What time of day does Charlie do these things? Match the activity to the time of day.

a. Wake up   Evening

b. Go to sleep   Afternoon

c. Eat lunch   Morning

DAYS OF THE WEEK

Peppermint Patty sometimes forgets the order of the days of the week and often turns up for sports practice on the wrong day!

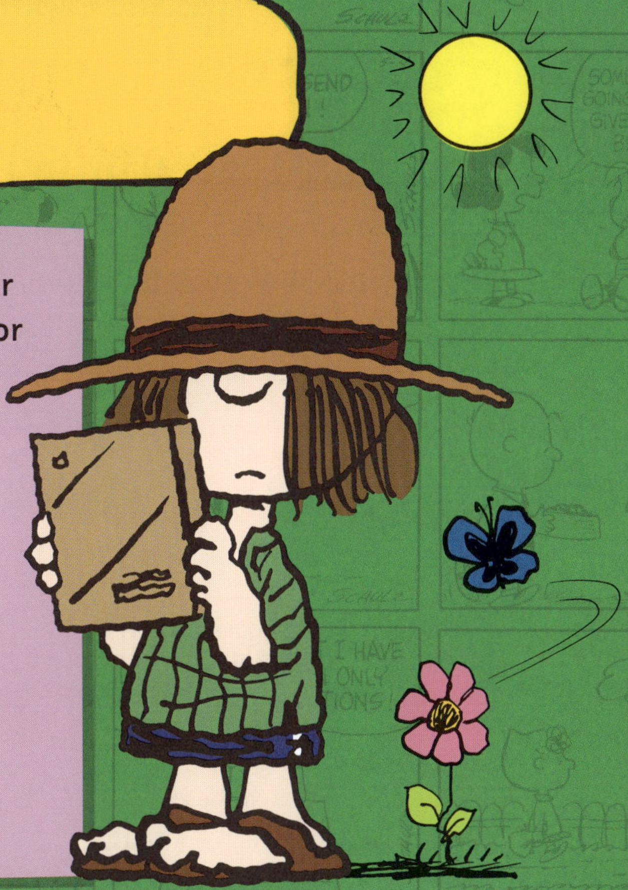

Peppermint Patty is trying to remember that the days of the week always go in the same order:

Monday
Tuesday
Wednesday
Thursday
Friday
Saturday ⎫
Sunday   ⎬ These two days are called the weekend.

1 Find the days of the week in this wordsearch.

d	a	y	a	t	h	u	r	s	d	a	y	m	d	y
s	u	n	s	u	n	d	e	r	m	o	d	f	r	i
p	e	t	n	e	r	t	e	o	o	g	h	z	c	a
o	g	o	l	s	x	w	e	d	n	e	s	d	a	y
l	h	k	g	d	j	q	a	x	d	b	f	n	l	j
d	t	l	s	a	t	u	r	d	a	y	c	r	d	f
t	h	u	u	y	z	z	s	f	y	p	t	n	i	q
s	a	q	n	f	g	t	o	d	a	y	a	m	d	k
f	r	i	d	a	y	p	a	o	k	m	t	l	a	r
g	t	w	a	v	o	s	a	t	t	c	z	f	y	t
u	n	n	y	v	p	o	e	n	o	d	a	y	n	t

☐ Monday
☐ Tuesday
☐ Wednesday
☐ Thursday
☐ Friday
☐ Saturday
☐ Sunday

2 Help Peppermint Patty by answering these questions.

a. What day comes after Thursday?
_____

b. How many days are in the week altogether?
_____

c. What day comes before Sunday?
_____

d. How many days are in the weekend?
_____

TELLING THE TIME

Charlie Brown is teaching Snoopy how to tell the time so that he knows when Charlie will be home from school.

1 Can you answer the questions below?

a. How many minutes are there in an hour? ☐

b. How many hours are there in a day? ☐

2 Draw a line to match these clocks to the correct time.

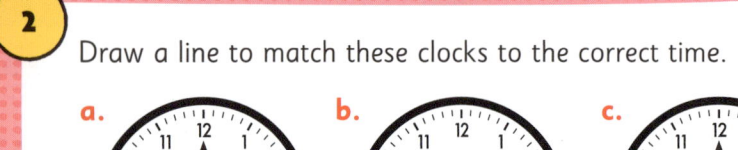

a.  Half past 4   b. 3 o'clock   c. 6 o'clock

3 Charlie knows Snoopy needs to be able to read the clock face to tell the time. Draw the hands on these clocks.

  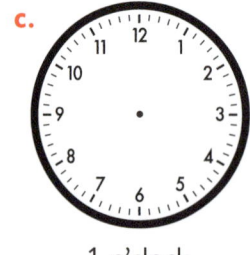

a. Half past 4   b. Quarter past 7   c. 1 o'clock

d. 3 o'clock   e. Half past 9   f. Quarter to 2

2D SHAPES

Miss Othmar is teaching Marcie and her friends about shapes.

The ball is a circle shape.

The present is a square shape.

Flat shapes are called 2D shapes.

      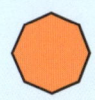 

square   circle   triangle   rectangle   pentagon   hexagon   octagon   oval

1 Match these shapes that Miss Othmar has drawn to their names.

a.    b.    c.    d.

pentagon   rectangle   triangle   circle

2 Have a go at labelling these shapes. You can use the shapes at the top of the page to help.

a. 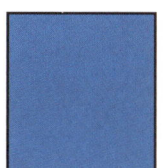   b.    c.    d.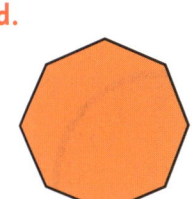

_____   _____   _____   _____

CORNERS AND SIDES

Christmas is coming and Sally is getting ready. She's written her Christmas cards and now she's addressing them. She's made stamps in lots of different 2D shapes to stick on the envelopes.

Different 2D shapes have a different number of sides and corners.

1 Label these shapes with the facts about their sides and corners.

a.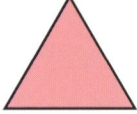

☐ corners ☐ sides

b.

☐ corners ☐ sides

c.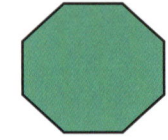

☐ corners ☐ sides

d.

☐ corners ☐ sides

e.

☐ corners ☐ sides

f.

☐ corners ☐ sides

2 Sally is trying to work out what shape this stamp is. Help her by matching each description to the correct name.

a. 4 corners and 4 equal sides   Triangle

b. 0 corners and 1 side   Square

c. 3 corners and 3 sides   Circle

3D SHAPES

It's Franklin's birthday and he's having a fancy dress party! He has been given lots of presents from his friends and they are all different shapes. These shapes aren't flat; he can pick them up so that means they are 3D shapes.

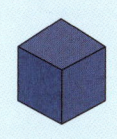

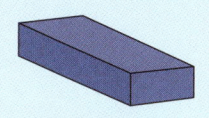

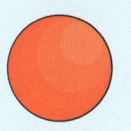

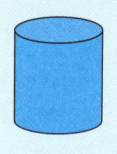

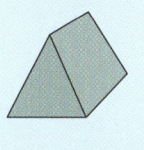

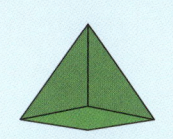

cube   cuboid   sphere   cylinder   triangular prism   cone   square-based pyramid

1

Help Franklin by naming the shapes.

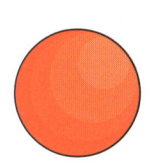

a.   b.   c.   d.

_____   _____   _____   _____

2

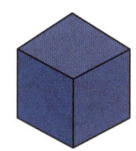

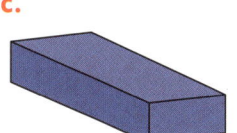

We use special words to describe the properties of 3D shapes.

Vertices is the plural of the word vertex, which is the point at which two or more edges meet. It is another word for corner.

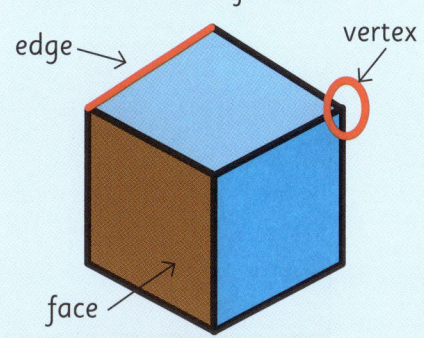

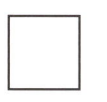

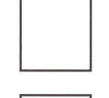

edge → vertex
face

		Number of faces	Number of edges	Number of vertices
a.	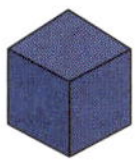	☐	☐	☐
b.	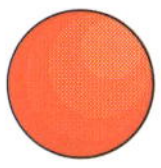	☐	☐	☐
c.	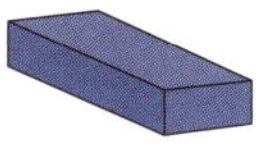	☐	☐	☐
d.		☐	☐	☐
e.		☐	☐	☐

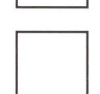

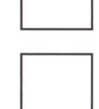

3D SHAPE NETS

Franklin is looking at his birthday presents, wondering what's inside the colourful gift boxes. He's noticed that he can see 2D shapes on the surface of the 3D shapes.

1

He has described some of the things he can see, can you help him by writing the name of the 3D shape?

| cube | square-based pyramid | sphere |

a. I can see four triangles and a square on this shape.

b. This shape has no 2D shapes that I can see, but when I see its shadow, it is a circle.

c. This shape has six square faces.

The shape is a _____

The shape is a _____

The shape is a _____

2

Franklin has flattened the 3D gift boxes into nets. Can you match the nets to the 3D shapes that they make?

A shape net shows what a 3D shape looks like if it's opened out flat.

a.   b.    c.

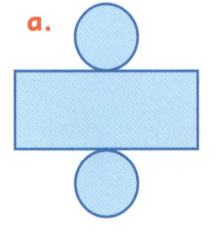

Cuboid   Cylinder   Cube

2D AND 3D SHAPES

Sally is using different shapes to build a house for her teddy. She knows that some are 2D and some are 3D but she doesn't know which are which!

1 Label the groups of shapes below to say if they are 2D or 3D.

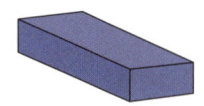

a. We can pick these shapes up. These are _____ shapes.

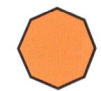

b. These shapes are flat. We call them _____ shapes.

2 These shapes have got all muddled up! Colour the 2D shapes in red, and the 3D shapes in green.

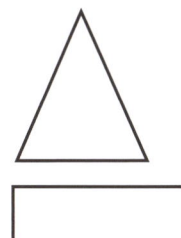

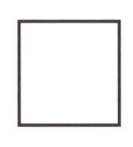

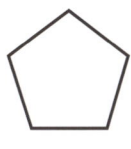

3 Sally has finished playing and has tidied the shapes. Has she done it correctly? Draw a circle around the odd ones out.

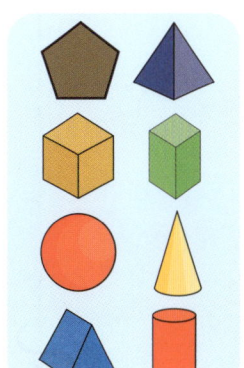

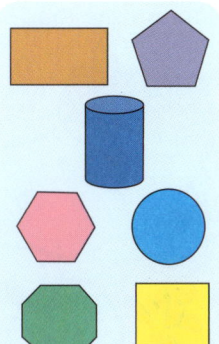

3D   2D

39

POSITION

Snoopy is imagining he's a pirate searching for hidden treasure. Can you help him find the gold?

1 Match each picture to the sentence that correctly describes where the treasure is by writing the correct letter in the box.

a.

b.

c.

Snoopy is **next** to the treasure chest. ☐

Snoopy is **behind** the treasure chest. ☐

Snoopy is in **front** of the treasure chest. ☐

2 Snoopy is so close to finding the treasure! Follow the instructions below to help him mark the locations on the map.

Draw an **X** in the top left square on the map.

Draw an **X** in the bottom right square on the map.

Draw an **X** in the middle square on the map.

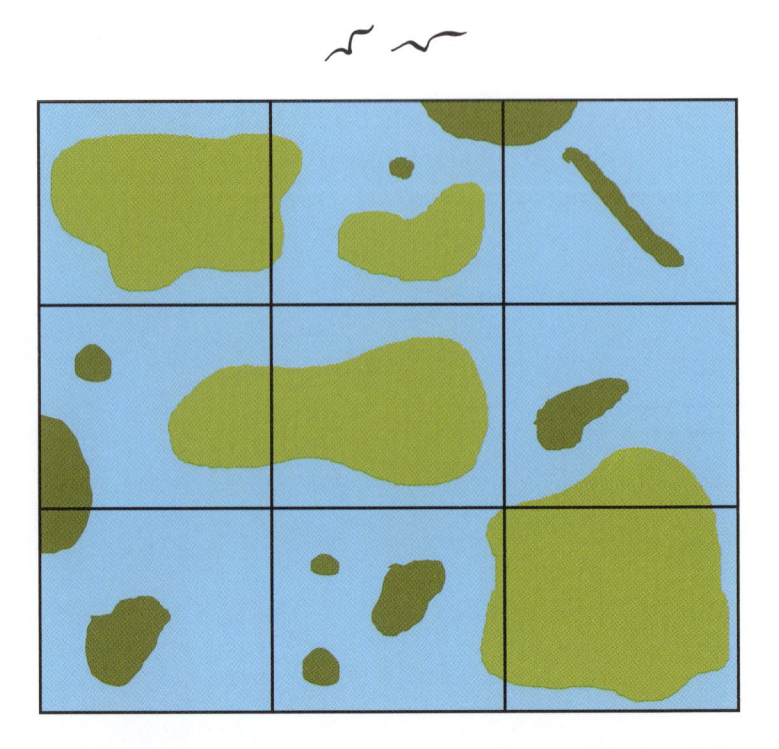

SHAPE PATTERNS

Sally is making colourful bracelets following a pattern. She knows that in a pattern, things take turns and the patterns repeat.

1 Have a go at completing these patterns by colouring in the rest of the boxes.

a.

b.

2 Complete these patterns by drawing the next 2 shapes.

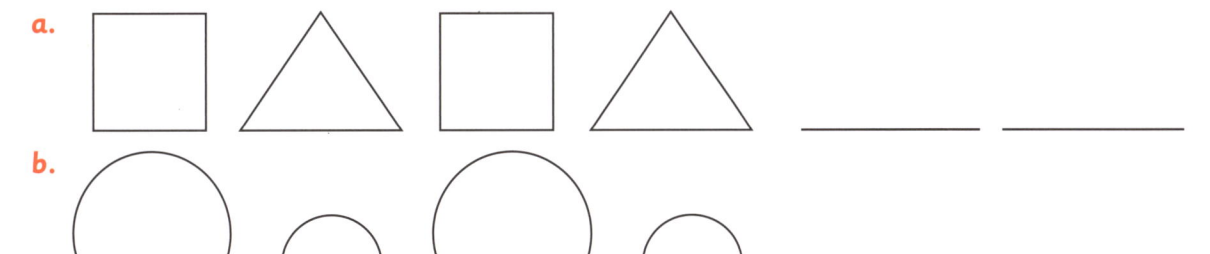

a.

b.

3 This bracelet is for Linus. Can you help Sally fill in the missing colours in the pattern?

Do you think Linus will like his present?

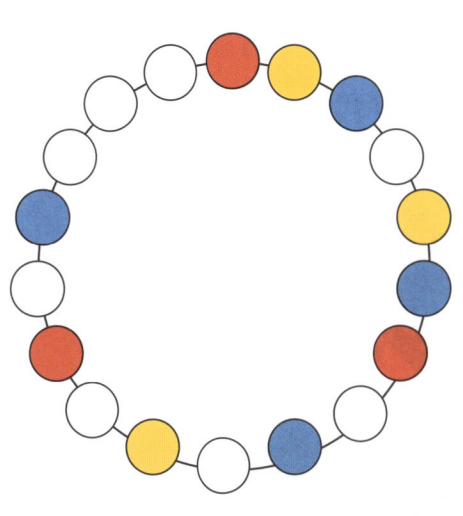

PATTERNS

Peppermint Patty is tidying up the sports equipment cupboard at school. She's found lots of numbered baseballs and wants to organise them into a pattern as she knows that you can make patterns with numbers as well as shapes and colours.

1 Odd numbers and even numbers are an example of patterns. Complete these number patterns with odd and even numbers.

a. 2, 4, ☐, 8, 10, ☐, 14, ☐, 18

b. 5, 7, 9, ☐, 13, 15, ☐, 19, ☐, 23, ☐, 27

2 Patterns can have different jumps between numbers. Have a go at completing these patterns. You need to see how much is added or subtracted between each jump and follow the same rule to find the missing numbers.

a. 3, 6, 9, 12, ☐, 18, 21, ☐, 27

b. 40, 35, ☐, 25, 20, ☐, 10

c. 11, 21, 31, ☐, 51, 61, ☐, 81

3 These patterns are already complete, but can you identify the rule? Look at what is added and subtracted between each step and write it in the box.

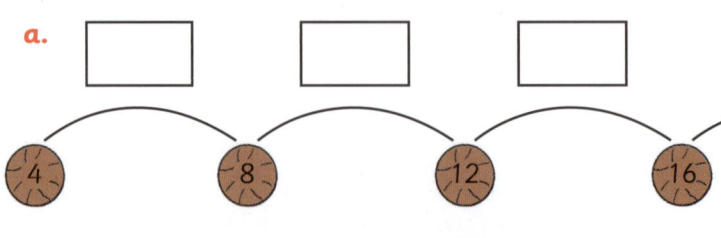

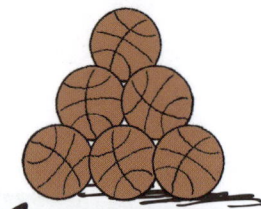

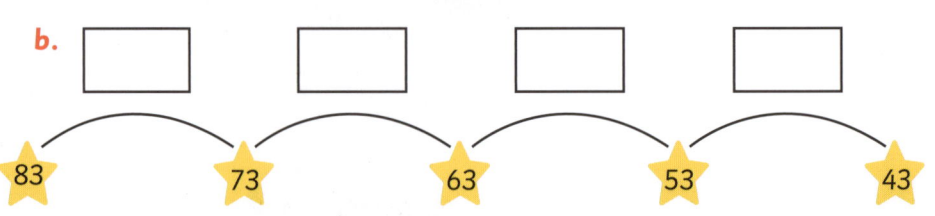

a. ☐ ☐ ☐ ☐
   4 — 8 — 12 — 16 — 20

b. ☐ ☐ ☐ ☐
   83 — 73 — 63 — 53 — 43

DIRECTION AND MOVEMENT

Charlie and Linus are on the bus to school but the driver is new and doesn't know the way. They need to give them some directions to follow. Can you help?

1 Look at the plan that the bus driver needs to follow and complete the instructions to get the children to school on time.

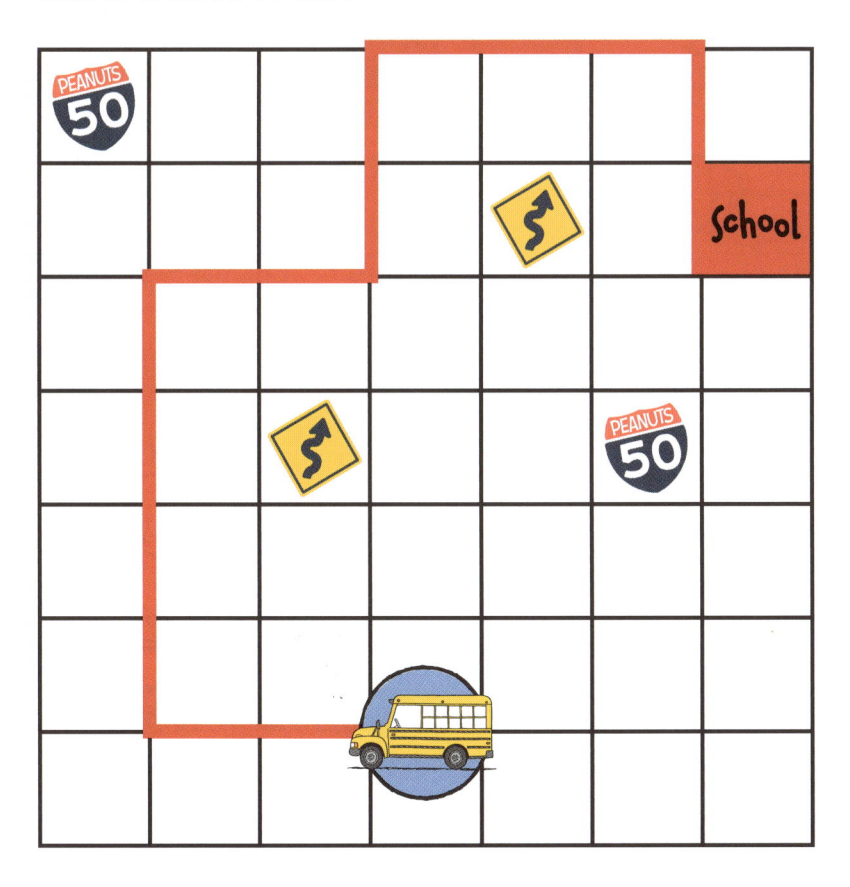

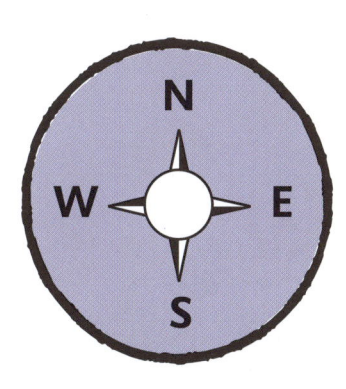

North

South

East

West

a. Move _____ 2 spaces.

b. Move _____ 4 spaces.

c. Move East _____ spaces.

d. Move North _____ spaces.

e. Move _____ 3 spaces.

f. Move South _____ space.

43

PICTOGRAMS AND TALLY CHARTS

Charlie and Sally are decorating the Brown family Christmas tree but Snoopy has managed to get the decorations in a muddle!

Help them count how many of each different decoration they have by making a tally chart. It is really easy to do, just make a vertical mark for the first 4 items that you count, and on the 5th item cross through the 4 lines.

Start again for the 6th item. You might find it helpful to cross the items out as you count them.

2

Sally has started a pictogram to show how many of each decoration they have. Can you use the results from your tally to finish it? Draw the correct number of each item onto the pictogram.

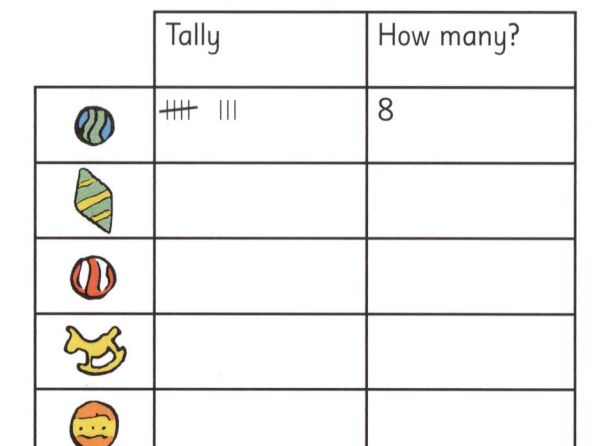

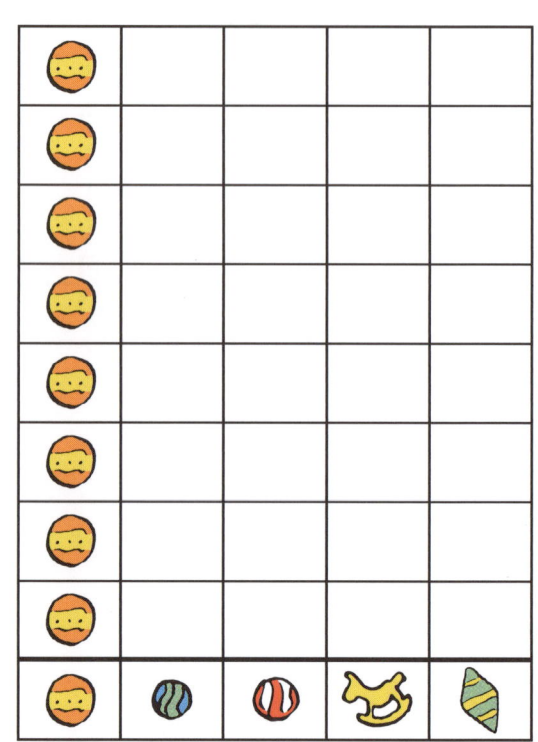

1

Charlie has had a go at starting this tally chart, can you finish it for him?

	Tally	How many?
🔵	|||| |||	8
🔶		
🔴		
🐴		
🟡		

44

BLOCK CHARTS AND TABLES

The Peanuts gang are having a jumble sale and everyone has a stall. Can you help count what they've sold so far?

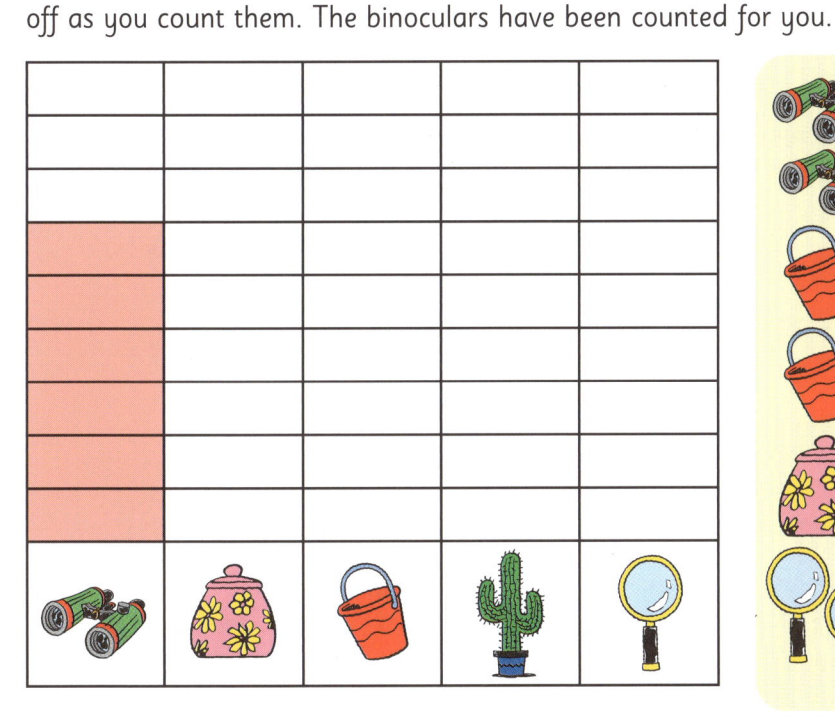

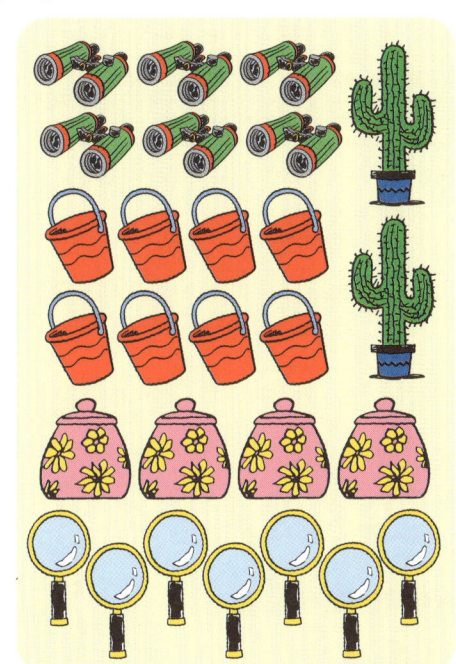

1 For every item you count, colour a box of the block chart in. It might help to cross the items off as you count them. The binoculars have been counted for you.

2 Charlie and Sally have put the money they've made at the jumble sale into piles so they can compare them. They've recorded their findings in a table.

	Height of Charlie's money	Height of Sally's money
10p coins	20cm	18cm
20p coins	15cm	11cm
£5 notes	36cm	16cm
£10 notes	19cm	17cm

Can you tick whether each of the statements below is true or false?

a. All of Charlie's piles of money are bigger than Sally's.   TRUE ☐   FALSE ☐

b. Sally's 20p pile is shorter than Charlie's 20p pile.   TRUE ☐   FALSE ☐

c. Charlie's £5 note pile is twice as tall as Sally's.   TRUE ☐   FALSE ☐

45

ANSWERS

Page 2: Numbers to 100
1.

1	2	3	4	5	6	7	8	9	10
11	12	13	14	15	16	17	18	19	20
21	22	23	24	25	26	27	28	29	30
31	32	33	34	35	36	37	38	39	40
41	42	43	44	45	46	47	48	49	50
51	52	53	54	55	56	57	58	59	60
61	62	63	64	65	66	67	68	69	70
71	72	73	74	75	76	77	78	79	80
81	82	83	84	85	86	87	88	89	90
91	92	93	94	95	96	97	98	99	100

2. a. 19, 28, 37, 48, 60
   b. 33, 41, 44, 52, 63, 72
   c. 55, 64, 66, 83, 94

Page 3: Counting
1. a. 5   b. 9   c. 12   d. 17
   11 - eleven, 4 - four
   8 - eight, 19 - nineteen
2. a. 20   c. 7   e. 5
   b. 11   d. 2   f. 14

Page 4: Counting
1. a. (hats)
   b. (shoes)
   c. (pink hats)
   d. (orange hats)
2. When completed in number order, the dot-to-dot shows a t-shirt.

Page 5: One more and one less
1. a. One more: 7, One less: 5
   b. One more: 9, One less: 7
   c. One more: 5, One less: 3
   d. One more: 6, One less: 4
2. a. 6   c. 20   e. 15
   b. 11   d. 0

Page 6: Comparing numbers
1. 1, 4, 8, 11, 19, 21
2. a. >   b. =   c. <   d. <   e. >

Page 7: Value of digits
1. a. 6 tens and 5 ones
   b. 4 tens and 2 ones
   c. 3 tens and 8 ones
   d. 1 ten and 3 ones
   e. 2 tens and 6 ones

2. a. 32   b. 75   c. 49   d. 51   e. 17
3. a. 34   b. 17   c. 25   d. 49

Page 8: Solving number problems
1. a. 13   b. 36   c. 33   d. 39
2. a. True   c. False   e. False
   b. False   d. True

Page 9: Adding and taking away to 10
1. a. 8   b. 10   c. 8
2. a. 2   b. 9   c. 4   d. 4
3. a. 3   b. 7   c. 2   d. 4

Page 10: Adding and taking away to 20
1. a. 19   c. 16   e. 1   g. 5
   b. 15   d. 12   f. 10   h. 9
2. a. 6 + 4 = 10 so 60 + 40 = 100
   b. 2 + 8 = 10 so 20 + 80 = 100
   c. 7 + 3 = 10 so 70 + 30 = 100
   d. 5 + 5 = 10 so 50 + 50 = 100
   e. 1 + 9 = 10 so 10 + 90 = 100

Page 11: Addition and subtraction
1. a. 10   b. 9   c. 11   d. 12
2. a. 3   b. 6   c. 4   d. 2

Page 12: Addition and subtraction
1. a. 9   b. 25   c. 15   d. 8   e. 9   f. 31
2. a. 12   b. 12   c. 8   d. 7   e. 4   f. 34

Page 13: Addition and subtraction
1. a. 17   c. 19   e. 23   g. 55   i. 63
   b. 18   d. 19   f. 56   h. 62   j. 46

Page 14: Part whole models
1. a. 6   b. 6   c. 9   d. 8
2. 19
3. 8
4. 18

Page 15: Finding the inverse
1. a. 3   b. 5   c. 12   d. 13   e. 5
2. a. 12 + 4 = 16, 4 + 12 = 16,
      16 - 4 = 12, 16 - 12 = 4
   b. 10 + 7 = 17, 7 + 10 = 17,
      17 - 7 = 10, 17 - 10 = 7
   c. 14 + 6 = 20, 6 + 14 = 20,
      20 - 6 = 14, 20 - 14 = 6

Page 16: Grouping and arrays
1. a. 9   b. 10   c. 8   d. 20   e. 20
2. a. 8   b. 9   c. 14   d. 10

Page 17: 2s, 5s and 10s
1. a. 4   b. 10   c. 6   d. 16   e. 8
2. a. 50   b. 35   c. 20   d. 45   e. 15
3. a. 8 x 10 = 80   d. 7 x 10 = 70
   b. 2 x 10 = 20   e. 3 x 10 = 30
   c. 5 x 10 = 50

Page 18: Odds and evens
1. a. 4, 10, 14, 16, 20
   b. 1, 5, 11, 13, 17
2. Odd: 6 and 12
   Even: 1, 11 and 7
3. When completed in number order, the odd numbers dot-to-dot shows an easel and the even numbers dot-to-dot shows a paintbrush.

Page 19: Multiplying and dividing
1. picture a: 4 x 2 = 8, 8 ÷ 2 = 4
   picture b: 5 x 5 = 25, 25 ÷ 5 = 5
   picture c: 3 x 3 = 9, 9 ÷ 3 = 3
   picture d: 7 x 3 = 21, 21 ÷ 3 = 7
   picture e: 6 x 3 = 18, 18 ÷ 3 = 6
   picture f: 3 x 2 = 6, 6 ÷ 2 = 3
   picture g: 3 x 5 = 15, 15 ÷ 5 = 3

Page 20: Multiplying and dividing
1. a. 3 x 4 = 12, 4 x 3 = 12
      12 ÷ 4 = 3, 12 ÷ 3 = 4
   b. 3 x 6 = 18, 6 x 3 = 18
      18 ÷ 6 = 3, 18 ÷ 3 = 6
   c. 2 x 10 = 20, 10 x 2 = 20
      20 ÷ 10 = 2, 20 ÷ 2 = 10
2. a. 12 ÷ 3 = 4
   b. 3 ÷ 1 = 3
   c. 21 ÷ 7 = 3

Page 21: Multiplication problems
1. a. 15   c. 40   e. 14   g. 90
   b. 100   d. 2   f. 6   h. 25
2. a. 3 x 3 = 9
   b. 2 x 4 = 8 or 4 x 2 = 8
   c. 4 x 10 = 40 or 10 x 4 = 40
   d. 5 x 2 = 10 or 2 x 5 = 10
3. a. 30 minutes
   b. 40 people
   c. 18 gloves

Page 22: Division problems
1. a. 4   d. 2   g. 5
   b. 7   e. 10   h. 9
   c. 6   f. 4   i. 3

2. 5
3. 5
4. 10
5. 5

Page 23: Finding a half
1.
2.

3. a. 2   b. 5   c. 3   d. 6

Page 24: Finding a quarter
1.
2.
3. a. 2   b. 4   c. 1   d. 3

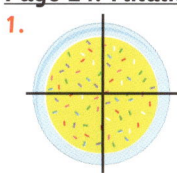

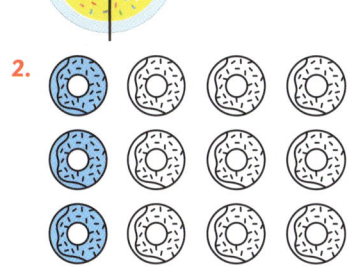

Page 25: Fractions of shapes
1.
2.
3.

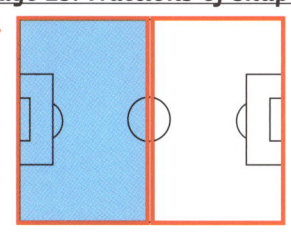

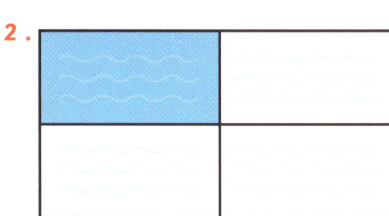

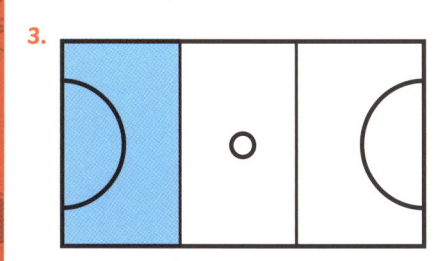

Page 26: Fractions of amounts
1. a. 5
   b. 2
   c. 4
   d. 6
   e. 2

f. 1
g. 2

2. a. 3   c. 4   e. 2
   b. 5   d. 8   f. 6

Page 27: Equivalent Fractions
1. a. 2   b. 3

   $\frac{1}{2} = \frac{2}{4}$ $\frac{1}{2} = \frac{3}{6}$

   c. 5 $\frac{1}{2} = \frac{5}{10}$

   d. 8 $\frac{1}{2} = \frac{8}{16}$

2.

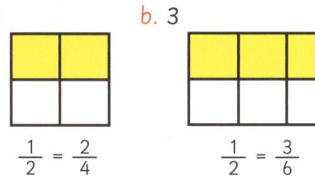

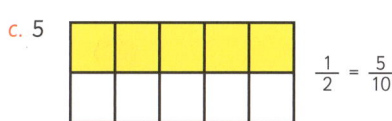

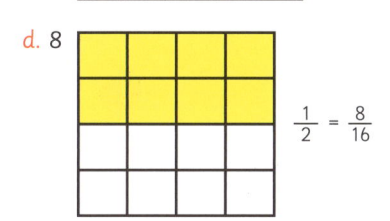

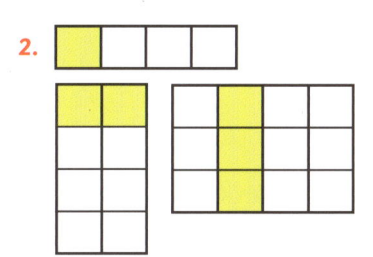

Page 28: Equivalent Fractions
1. a. 2   b. 4   c. 1   d. 6   e. 2   f. 1
2. a. $\frac{1}{2}$ $\frac{4}{8}$ c. $\frac{2}{5}$ $\frac{4}{10}$
   b. $\frac{2}{3}$ $\frac{4}{6}$ d. $\frac{1}{4}$ $\frac{3}{12}$
3. a. $\frac{1}{2}$ b. $\frac{1}{4}$ c. $\frac{3}{4}$

Page 29: Measuring
1. a. Shorter   b. Longer
2. a. Shorter   b. Taller
3. a. Lighter   b. Heavier

Page 30: Comparing Measurements
1. 4cm   2. 5cm
3. The red gift box is wider
4. a. 100g   b. 400g   c. Yes

Page 31: Money
1. 1, d
   2, a
   3, b
   4, c
2. a. 85p   b. 70p   c. 95p

Page 32: Ordering events in a day
1.

2. a. Wake up - morning
   b. Go to sleep - evening
   c. Eat lunch - afternoon

Page 33: Days of the week
1.

2. a. Friday   c. Saturday
   b. 7   d. 2

Page 34: Telling the time
1. a. 60   b. 24
2. a. 6 o'clock   c. 3 o'clock
   b. Half past 4
3. a.   d.
   b.   e.
   c.   f.

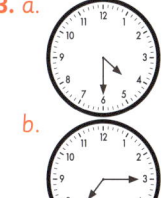

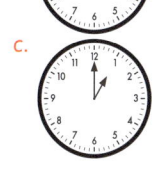

Page 35: 2D Shapes
1. a. circle   c. rectangle
   b. triangle   d. pentagon
2. a. square   c. hexagon
   b. oval   d. octagon

Page 36:
Corners and Sides

1. a. 3 corners, 3 sides
   b. 4 corners, 4 sides
   c. 8 corners, 8 sides
   d. 5 corners, 5 sides
   e. 0 corners, 1 sides
   f. 4 corners, 4 sides

2. a. square   b. circle   c. triangle

Page 37: 3D Shapes

1. a. sphere   c. cuboid
   b. cube   d. cylinder

2. a. 6 faces, 12 edges, 8 vertices
   b. 1 faces, 0 edges, 0 vertices
   c. 6 faces, 12 edges, 8 vertices
   d. 3 faces, 2 edges, 0 vertices
   e. 2 faces, 1 edges, 1 vertex

Page 38: 3D Shape nets

1. a. square-based pyramid
   b. sphere
   c. cube

2. a. cylinder   b. cube   c. cuboid

Page 39: 2D and 3D shapes

1. a. 3D   b. 2D
2.
3. 3D   2D

Page 40: Position

1. a. Snoopy is in front of the treasure chest.
   b. Snoopy is behind the treasure chest.
   c. Snoopy is next to the treasure.
2.

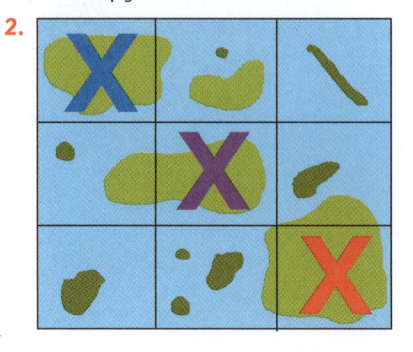

Page 41: Shape patterns

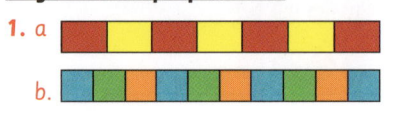

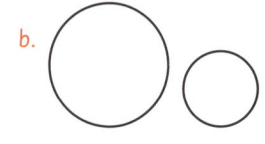

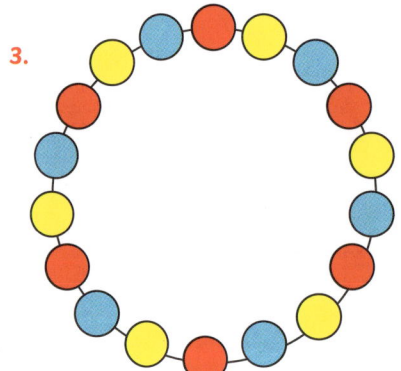

1. a.
   b.
2. a.
   b.
3.

Page 42: Patterns

1. a. 6, 12, 16   b. 11, 17, 21, 25
2. a. 15, 24   b. 30, 15   c. 41, 71
3. a. + 4, + 4. + 4, + 4
   b. −10, −10, −10, −10

Page 43: Direction and movement

1. a. Move West 2 spaces.
   b. Move North 4 spaces.
   c. Move East 2 spaces.
   d. Move North 2 spaces.
   e. Move East 3 spaces.
   f. Move South 1 space.

Page 44: Pictograms and tally charts

1.
	Tally	How many?
										8
				2
							5
					3
										8

2.

Page 45: Block charts and tables

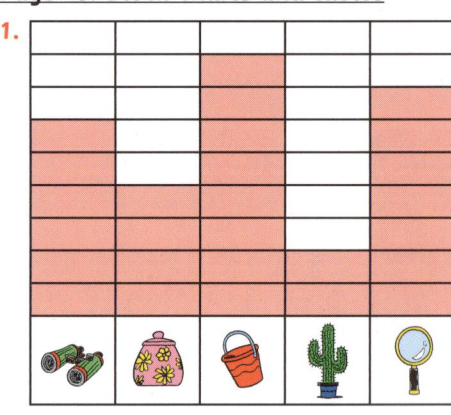

1.
2. a. True   b. True   c. False